D1715137

MAKE MONEY EASY

ALSO BY LEWIS HOWES

*The Greatness Mindset: Unlock the Power
of Your Mind and Live Your Best Life Today**

*The School of Greatness: A Real-World Guide to
Living Bigger, Loving Deeper, and Leaving a Legacy*

*The Mask of Masculinity: How Men
Can Embrace Vulnerability, Create Strong
Relationships, and Live Their Fullest Lives*

*Available from Hay House

Please visit:
Hay House USA: www.hayhouse.com
Hay House Australia: www.hayhouse.com.au
Hay House UK: www.hayhouse.co.uk
Hay House India: www.hayhouse.co.in

MAKE MONEY EASY

CREATE FINANCIAL FREEDOM AND LIVE A RICHER LIFE

Lewis Howes

HAY HOUSE LLC
Carlsbad, California · New York City
London · Sydney · New Delhi

Published in the United States by: Hay House LLC, www.hayhouse.com®
P.O. Box 5100, Carlsbad, CA, 92018-5100

Cover design: Chris Allen • *Interior design:* Julie Davison
Interior illustrations: StoryBuilders

Cataloging-in-Publication Data is on file at the Library of Congress

Hardcover ISBN: 978-1-4019-9393-1
E-book ISBN: 978-1-4019-9394-8

10 9 8 7 6 5 4 3 2 1
1st edition, March 2025

Printed in the United States of America

This product uses responsibly sourced papers and/or recycled materials. For more information, see www.hayhouse.com.

The authorized representative in the EU for product safety and compliance is Penguin Random House Ireland, Morrison Chambers, 32 Nassau Street, Dublin D02 YH68, Ireland. https://eu-contact.penguin.ie

I dedicate this book to the child in me who watched in wonder as my father tipped with $2 bills which reminds me of the uniqueness we all bring to the world. Keep enduring the highs and lows, the gains and losses of mental, emotional and financial freedom.

CONTENTS

Disclaimer: I believe in you and in the power of "financial freedom" and "living a richer life," but I also recognize that these concepts are deeply personal and mean different things to each of us. I encourage you to think of this book as the beginning of your journey to understand your relationship with money and explore what these concepts mean for you. What resonates with me might not resonate with you, and that's perfectly okay!

My intent is not to promise specific outcomes but to inspire, inform, and empower you to become more. Any stories I share from my past experiences are unique to me and your stories and results will vary and be unique to you. The information I share is solely for informational purposes and should not be considered financial or legal advice. If you want tailored guidance, I recommend seeking specific advice from professionals who can help you achieve your own financial goals in your unique circumstances.

I'm excited to support you on your journey to living a richer life!

INTRODUCTION

I stole things. A lot of things. It's not something I'm proud of now, but as I headed into my teen years, I almost became a kleptomaniac. Now, I wasn't robbing banks or stealing expensive things, but I used the same talent I had for visualizing and anticipating where empty spaces were on the sports fields and basketball courts to scope out stores, gas stations, and restaurants.

It sort of became a game for me. I'd walk into a place and see where they had double-sided mirrors, where cameras were installed, and how close I was to the nearest employee. I felt like an invincible magician, using sleight of hand as I palmed candy bars, buying one as I slipped another into my pocket. I didn't even smoke, but I stole cigarettes *just because I could.*

I truly believed I would never get caught. And I didn't—until the day I stole from one of my dad's clients. My dad sold life insurance for around thirty years to make a living for our family. He worked extremely hard, often late at night and on weekends, to always do right by his clients. One day after basketball practice, he took one of my teammates and me to a client's farmhouse near our place in Ohio. As they sat at the kitchen table doing business, my friend and I gave ourselves a tour of the house.

When we got to the basement, a knowing glance passed between us. We began pulling on the cold metal knobs of the desk drawers, shuffling through papers to see what we could find. Then we found our prize—*twenty-five bucks*! I must have been feeling generous because I handed my friend the twenty and kept the five for myself. We slowly slid the drawers shut and crept back upstairs, feeling pretty pumped about our find—at least until the middle of the night.

A bright light suddenly shone in my face, causing me to sit straight up in bed. My father's larger-than-life frame hovered over me, demanding to know if I took money from his client. "No," was my bleary-eyed reply. "I didn't take anything." Bad move. Dad had already called my friend's parents, and he had admitted everything to them.

Later that morning we took an hour-long drive back to the farmhouse with the stolen cash in my hand. We rode in silence, but I could feel my dad's anger emanating from the driver's seat. I still remember how ashamed I felt when we got out of the car and stepped toward the farmer. My father had told me the farmer had gone to buy feed for his livestock, opened his wallet, and realized he didn't have enough money. I imagined him then going home empty-handed to face his family. I still remember how ashamed I felt when we got out of the car and stepped toward the farmer. When I handed the money back to him, he just glared at me as he snatched it from my thieving little hand. It was one of the worst days of my life to that point.

As I look back now, I realize my choice to take the money created a ripple effect of negativity—my dad couldn't trust me, his client quit working with him, and I held on to the anger my dad felt and let it shape how I viewed money, even as an adult.

So what's the deal with money? Why do some people seem to have calm energy around it with no worries about how much they have or what they spend? Why do others have great anxiety about money and seem unwilling to spend it on anything? They obsessively check their banking app to track every last cent. Some people are buried in debt. Others seem just fine being clueless about how many credit cards they have and never even check their bank balances.

They say money doesn't buy happiness. But neither does poverty. I've been broke and depressed. But I've also been broke and happy, and I've seen genuinely happy people in some of the poorest places in the world.

I've had a lot of money and been miserable, and I've been around a lot of wealthy people with unhealthy and broken lives. On the other hand, I've also had what most people would call a lot of money and felt deeply fulfilled. And I've also spent time with ultra-wealthy people and seen healthy, loving, abundantly generous lives of bliss and complete freedom. Suffice it to say, your happiness in life doesn't directly correlate to how much money you have.

All of it can leave you feeling that money is, well . . . complicated.

For most of us, everything we've been told about money is wrong. For example, people often have an emotional connection to money. I know I do. In fact, it may be the most important *intimate* relationship you *didn't* know you had. Whether you know it or not, you already have a relationship with money. And until you heal your relationship with money, nothing can change for the better. Because if you don't care for your money, your money won't care for you.

We learn how to create a relationship with money in the same way we figured out how to interact with other people when we were children—observation and experience. Our minds interpret what we notice about our parents, older family members, and others we encounter as they interact with money. It's tough to try to repair a relationship with another person, let alone with something as complicated as money. But the longer you ignore the fact that your relationship with money could use some improvements, the worse it gets. Most of us, whether we know it or not, have some type of money trauma, and this impacts our money story and our money style today. All of this impacts our sense of self-worth and self-confidence, and even our very identity, if we let it.

Truth be told, I think a lot of people have simply given up trying to figure money out. No matter what they do, something just feels off. They suspect that much of their future happiness depends on money, but think money is supposed to be an old friend, even if it more often feels like a total stranger they just met on a dating app. Something feels both familiar and foreign about it all at the same time.

For one thing, we have a financial literacy problem. It isn't only that so many of us don't know much about money; we don't even know what we don't know. And it shows. More than three in four Americans say they live paycheck to paycheck. Another one in four say they haven't saved anything for retirement, and at least one in five don't have emergency savings.[1]

Unfortunately, most of us simply weren't instructed about how to be wise with money. Not only do we not understand how to have a healthy relationship with it, but we also just haven't been taught what to do with it at all. We are expected to either wing it or figure it out somewhere between high school and college. And we aren't given the tools to prepare us to pay our own taxes, understand how to avoid credit card debt, or properly invest our money.

Money plays an important role in securing a safe and comfortable life, but without the proper tools and training, people end up stuck. From an early age, kids learn most of what they do know about money from their parents. But if the family treats money as a "hush-hush" topic of conversation like it was in my family, then kids go into the world unaware of what money can do *to* or *for* them.

I wrote this book because I wanted to learn more about my own money blocks and see how I could break through to having a more secure relationship with money. Most people struggle their entire lives around money issues, and it directly impacts every personal relationship we are in if we don't learn how to have a healthy experience with it.

On my show *The School of Greatness*, I've been blessed over the last decade to interview and connect with some of the world's wealthiest people, those who came from nothing and made millions of dollars, and those who have lost it all. I've also met a lot of wealthy people who are unhappy and don't have a good relationship with money. They still believe they will lose it all, or all people want from them is money, so they don't feel they can trust people. It becomes more stressful than peaceful. All of these individuals have shared their secrets with me about what to do and not to do with money, and most importantly, how not to let money control your life.

If you are a prisoner in your relationship with money, you will always feel trapped in life. If you set yourself free in your relationship with money, you may open yourself to becoming rich beyond your wildest dreams—and I'm not just talking about financial riches. Because, in my opinion, money is not what matters most in life; however, money can be a means to accessing and enhancing all the things that truly do matter most to you.

So if you've ever wondered, *Why does this money thing need to be so hard? Why can't I just make money easy?* I have two pieces of good news. First, you are not alone. We all feel the struggle. Second, you *can* heal your relationship with money to make it easier. I'll show you how.

At the end of the day, my goal for you is to help make money easy in your own life, so you can feel free and abundant. Because that is your birthright—to live a worthy, joyful life, and never to let money rob you of your peace.

STEP 1

Know Your Money Story

Growth begins with self-awareness. But far too many people never pause to become aware of how they interact with money. They just use it without thinking about what it is, why they engage with it in the way that they do, or how they might be naturally wired to think about it.

But if you want to make your relationship with money easy for you, you need to discover your own Money Story. That's Step 1, and it starts now.

Find more free resources to accelerate your growth and make money easy at MakeMoneyEasyBook.com.

CHAPTER ONE

THE TRUTH ABOUT MONEY

I guess you could say I grew up in a middle-class family. We had enough money to survive, and we always had food to eat and clothes to wear, but there always seemed to be a lack of peace in my home. And a lot of things, like fear, insecurity, and pain, got amplified when they involved money.

As a child, I didn't really understand the concept of money. No one really talked about it with me. The topic was so "hush-hush" in my family that it left me feeling like it was a bad thing when people had it. What I did learn was we didn't have much, so we needed to save and pay attention to what we spent. If I wanted money, I could ask my parents, and they would either give it to me or not.

When I turned 10, my parents gave me a small allowance of about $5 a week, but nothing consistent and usually only when I worked for it. They paid me for household chores like making my bed or putting away my laundry. This practice continued into my early teens, but I still had no clue how to get people other than my parents to pay me. It was scary to want more money when no one talked about it. I didn't know how to start a conversation about it, and I worried about how I would make it work when I got older.

Fast-forward a decade or so, and my Money Story continued to evolve. In my early twenties, I didn't have an entrepreneurial bone in my body. I also didn't have any cash, and my dream of playing professional football faded away when I received a career-ending wrist injury.

At that point, I had no full-time job experience. I had trained as an athlete, which paid a little playing in the Arena Football League, but I hoped it would pay off more one day if I could make it to the National Football League. My dad graciously paid for all my training and some of my college education, and I also managed to get some scholarships and take out student loans for the rest. The only job experience I had was working part-time as a paperboy, a greens mower at a golf course, a truck driver, and a club bouncer on weekends in college.

But when I was 22 years old, my dad experienced a devastating car accident that left him in a coma for months, then disabled and in recovery for 17 years until he passed. As he fought to get better, medical bills began to add up. My parents had divorced when I was 16. My dad's girlfriend at the time of the accident had power of attorney and decided it was best to sell my dad's life insurance business. A part of me felt ashamed for thinking it, but I realized I couldn't lean on him to give me money anymore. Plus, I had lost the safety-net idea of possibly going to work with him if necessary.

My family experienced so much kindness from others during that time. Several of my dad's employees gave me cards containing money to help out. I felt so grateful for their generosity, feeling a little sense of peace for a little while. But that money only lasted a few days, and then I was back to having nothing again.

Being broke meant I couldn't afford my own apartment. For almost a year and a half, my sister let me live rent-free on her couch. If I wanted to go out, I had to rely on the generosity of my friends and family to pay for my meals and entertainment. I hated how I felt when others paid for me.

But I kept moving forward, not sure what might materialize or how. I felt my physical health beginning to slip and my emotional health along with it.

As I sat in the car one day, I asked myself: *Why am I feeling unfulfilled? Why do I not feel satisfied when I've been so driven for the last several years? I've been goal-oriented and gotten things done, but now I don't feel fulfilled inside. Why?* As I shared in my book *The Greatness Mindset*, I needed to find my Meaningful Mission so I could once again become excited about being me.

While I was searching for new opportunities to find a job or make money, I reached out to a mentor of mine who suggested getting on LinkedIn. After months of exploring the platform, I learned I had an ability to connect with people in a powerful way. That platform was still in its early years, and people had a lot of questions about how to maximize it for career advancement. So I stepped up and began helping people for free. As more people found out how I had helped others, I started charging them for my services. I stumbled forward for several years, making progress some days and feeling like I fell short on others. Fast-forward a few years of learning, developing, and adding value to people, not only on LinkedIn but with social media in general, and I made my first million dollars in sales.

I was elated! Now, it didn't happen overnight. It required taking risks and working nonstop for most days. And what happened for me was my own personal experience, so your path will look different for you. At the time, I didn't think that this was my ultimate Meaningful Mission, but it was something I was excited about. I was learning new skills, helping others overcome challenges, and improving my financial situation in the process.

In more than a decade since that time, I've worked my way through a lot more growth phases concerning money and now have my own company with a clear Meaningful Mission: to serve 100 million people weekly by helping them improve the quality of their lives and overcome the things that hold them back. My show, *The School of Greatness*, continues to grow as one of the most popular podcasts in the world with amazing guests from whom I have learned so much. I've written two *New York Times* best-selling books and have gone from making nothing to making seven and eight figures annually now for many years.

By no means am I the richest person in the world, and I know more people than I can count who make way more than I do. I am not here to say I have mastered the money journey, but through decades of personal experience, plus years of interviewing the top financial experts and some of the wealthiest people in the world, I've made some key realizations and learned important habits.

One of the first realizations that has been key for me wasn't figuring out how to beat the stock market or discovering the latest real estate investing tips. All that has its place, but my most important lesson about money came to me when I was feeling the overwhelming stress of having nothing. In my early twenties, I looked to one of my mentors and friends, Chris Hawker, and blurted, "Man, I could really use some money right now."

And then Chris said this: "Money comes to you when you're ready for it."

I vividly remember my immediate response. "I feel pretty ready to make some money *right now*! It would really help me pay for rent and food. I can't buy clothes or gas—any of that stuff."

However, looking back a couple of years later, I realized I *wasn't* ready for money then. If the money had come to me, I probably wouldn't have had it for long. I needed to work on myself first to prepare myself to receive money. And so I did. It didn't happen suddenly; it was a process that took several years and, to be honest, is still happening within me every day.

But when I embraced this simple truth about money, everything began to change: to have more money, you must prepare to receive it.

To have more money, you must prepare to receive it.

— Lewis Howes

START LOOKING WITHIN

The counterintuitive reality is that when you focus on *who you are* and what unique value you can bring in service to the rest of the world, instead of *what money will give you*, your energy and actions actually invite more money into your life.

You—yes, *you*—are the key to making more money. I know life might have you feeling broken, but with the right awareness and tools, I believe you can start to remember who you are. You are whole. You are complete. My friend, you are enough. But you may not always feel this way, and my intention is to show you how to feel that way for those times when you feel empty or broken.

But first, it might be helpful to understand what money is and isn't—and your relationship with it.

Here is what money is *not*:

- **Money is not your savior.** No matter how much you want it to, money isn't going to save you from your current situation. It's not going to swoop in just in the nick of time to save you from mistakes you've made or help you sleep better at night. It can't make your relationships work or keep your family together. And it won't give you a sense of inner peace and fulfillment.

- **Money is not your enemy.** Money isn't out to get you. It's not laughing in the corner of the room when you sit down to try to figure out how you're going to pay the bills. It isn't the bully from middle school who hangs out with everyone else but you. It doesn't force you into a crazy game of hide-and-seek as the sneaky all-time hider leaving you as the frantic all-time seeker. If you view money as being against you, why would it ever come to you?

- **Money is not avoidable.** Some of us, probably all of us, have what I call money wounds. We've experienced some level of trauma in life that is connected with money in some way. But unlike other sources of trauma in life, we can't simply avoid money. We need it to live.

So if it isn't any of those things, what is money?

- **Money is an amplifier.** Money amplifies who you already are. That's great news *if* you are committed to becoming the very best version of you.

- **Money is a game.** Like any game, your experience with money should be fun. Whenever you try to do anything new, you shouldn't expect to be good at it at first. But as you progress in your skills, you can level up.

- **Money is energy.** Money has an energy and flow to it. It comes and goes. The tighter you hold on to it, the less it comes to you. The more you're willing to invest it, wisely spend it, and let it flow into the world, the more it will flow back to you. It's important to learn how to be in alignment with the flow of money at each season of life.

- **Money is a resource.** Money makes things possible for you and those you care about. It brings options and freedom to make choices you otherwise would not have had.

Money only becomes "the root of all evil" when you start letting it shape who you are. Because I put in the work to heal my relationship with money—an ongoing journey that continues to this day—I have learned how to get to a place of inner peace and understand my self-worth without tying it to my net worth.

I find it helpful to think about it with something I call the Financial Freedom Framework, which shows the relationship between having money and not having money, and enjoying a sense of freedom and peace and not feeling free or peaceful.

	Freedom	No Freedom
Money	**1** **Empowered** (See money as a friend.)	**2** **Frustrated** (See money as a failure.)
No Money	**3** **Happy** (See money as a restriction.)	**4** **Hopeless** (See money as an enemy.)

Let's work through each quadrant and see if any of these resonate with you.

Quadrant 1. People who do have money and enjoy a sense of peace and freedom in life tend to feel *empowered*. Not only do they feel fulfilled, but they have access to options to spread that freedom to others and make the world a better place. These people come to see money as a friend.

Quadrant 2. People who do have money but do not enjoy a sense of peace and freedom tend to feel *frustrated*. After all, they thought money would bring satisfaction, but they just aren't feeling fulfilled. They often come to see money as a failure, something that promised but didn't deliver.

Quadrant 3. People who have little or no money but do enjoy a sense of peace and freedom tend to feel *happy* for the most part. But their options for spreading that happiness are limited by their lack of money. As a result, they may see money as a restriction.

Quadrant 4. People who have little or no money and no sense of peace and freedom tend to feel *hopeless*. They often embrace a victim mentality, thinking there just isn't anything they can do to make money, so they often look to others to give it to them. In fact, they often tend to see money as an enemy.

My desire is that you move toward that first quadrant and begin to think of money as your friend. You wouldn't try to become friends with people just to use them, would you? You wouldn't want your friends to try to turn you into something you don't want to be, right? So why do we tend to let our relationship with money do that to us?

Your relationship with money may not be a friendly one at the moment, but wisdom tells us that the best way to attract friends is to prepare yourself to be the kind of person other friends—like money—actually want to be around. When you do the internal work and heal your relationship with money, you'll make a new friend who can come and go freely as you live a life with more peace and less stress.

3 CRITICAL STEPS TO IMPROVE YOUR RELATIONSHIP WITH MONEY

My intention is to help you create a better relationship with money from the inside out. As we move along your path to that healthier, more abundant relationship, I'm excited to be able to share stories from my own life along with incredible insights from financial experts I've hosted on *The School of Greatness* show.

But a word of caution: This book isn't filled with tips and tricks on how to become an overnight millionaire. And you're not about to learn the best ways to create an investment portfolio or dive into specific strategies to make your money work for you. It's important to consult with a financial advisor or professional for advice tailored to your specific circumstances. Instead, our focus will be on preparing yourself to receive money by working on *yourself* first.

Step 1: Know Your Money Story. We'll first explore your Money Story, unpack what that is, how it has been shaped, and how it shapes your own relationship with money. We'll explore some of the common struggles people have with money so you can see what resonates with you.

We'll see how each of us is uniquely wired to approach money differently, and you'll discover your own unique Money Style. Then we'll go deep to apply relationship insights to your own Money Style to really bring clarity to how you view money so you can start to make your relationship with money easier in your life.

Step 2: Reset Your Money Mindset. Then we'll explore what it means to heal your money wounds, the trauma associated with money in your Money Story. When you get rid of the things that are holding you back, you'll stop chasing the things you want and start attracting them instead. We'll discover exactly how you can become someone who attracts money to you. We'll connect money to your Meaningful Mission and explore how best to monetize it.

Step 3: Prepare for More Money. With a healthy foundation laid for reimagining your relationship with money, it's time to get practical and explore the 7 Money Habits.

- *Habit 1: The Mindset Habit*

  The counterintuitive truth about money is that the more generous you are with it, the more it tends to come back to you and the more positive energy you generate. And the more you manifest it, the more inspired you become to give it away.

- *Habit 2: The Mapping Habit*

  You can't get to your destination if you don't know where you're going. It's time to map out your life and make a money plan that you can work on day-to-day.

- *Habit 3: The Monetizing Habit*

  When you understand and appreciate your value, you can monetize it to share with the world. Unfortunately, too many people undervalue their unique gifts and skills. But not you. Not after deploying this habit.

- *Habit 4: The Mastermind Habit*

  Your connections can be the catalyst for your financial success if you go about it in the right way. I'll show you how I do it so you can seek your best money mentors, teachers, and friends who align with your mission.

- *Habit 5: The Magnetic Habit*

  When you get good at enrolling others in your money vision, you can multiply your ability to make money. I'll show you the secret for doing it well without feeling like you are intruding as you amplify who you are, genuinely help others, and grow your personal brand.

- *Habit 6: The Mobility Habit*

  To scale your ability to make money, you'll need to be able to move in your areas of greatest strengths. What the truly successful have learned to do well is to delegate everything else. I'll share how to mobilize your team to get more done and add more value to others.

- *Habit 7: The Mastery Habit*

  To keep your financial abundance and peace growing, you'll want to grow your financial knowledge. When you make learning about money part of the flow of your life, you may find money management much easier and more rewarding.

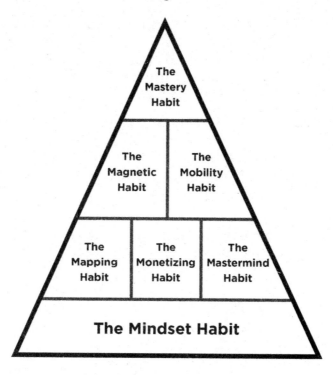

Understanding your Money Style will shape the type of relationship you have with money and directly correlate to how much money you make and how much peace, clarity, and freedom you will have for the rest of your life.

When you picked up this book, you took a huge first step. I'm excited to share what I've learned from incredible people, along with the financial insights and helpful habits I've used over the years. But believe me when I say that the most authentic foundation for a financially fulfilling life is to believe in yourself.

Now if you're ready to lean in, learn more, go deep, and take imperfect action, then you're ready to discover how to *Make Money Easy.*

CHAPTER TWO

YOUR MONEY STORY

I'll never forget the day it happened. It was the day after Father's Day. As I headed home after some time away, I cruised along, tapping my fingers on the steering wheel to the beat of a song. It was sunny and bright—just a regular day in L.A. Until it wasn't.

I pulled around the corner, heading toward my apartment building, and came to a full stop. Sheer chaos. Flashing lights from police and emergency vehicles reflected off a white tent. The sirens weren't blaring, but the sounds of urgent commands and shuffling feet pulled the song right out of my mind as I tried to catch up to the story developing before my eyes. Officers and paramedics moved through the scene as the feeling in the air alternated between busyness and shocked stillness.

After I pulled up and started asking questions, I was stunned to learn that a man had taken his own life by jumping out of the apartment building I was living in. And even more stunned when I heard his name.

Now, I won't try to pretend I knew much more about this man than his name and which apartment had been his. I had no clue about all the darkness he felt surrounding him during those last moments of his life. Having worked with mental health professionals on my journey of healing, my heart went out to him and his family. I understand the impact of trauma and abuse on my life, and if you're feeling out of options and overwhelmed with your current situation, I urge you to get help. I can tell you that I'm a different person after choosing to get help from professionals.

When I think about this man and the way his life ended so suddenly, I can't possibly explain why this happened. I cannot speculate about his relationships with family, friends, or business acquaintances. But one thing I do know about him is that he had money. He was known to have a few hundred million dollars in the bank. Yet even with all that money, this man was dealing with things that made him feel the only thing he could do that day was to leave this world and everything in it. And he isn't alone.

If you are confused by the relationship between money and mental health, know this: no matter how much or how little they have, the relationship people have with their money wounds is real.

MONEY LIES

I once asked my social media audience this question: "What's the biggest challenge you face that keeps you from making more money and being happy with your income?" Their top responses merit a deeper look because they simply are not true. See if any of these lies sound familiar to you:

- **Lack of training.** You may have chosen not to go to college, and now you feel like you should have, or vice versa. You start thinking that if you had gone to this college instead of that one, you'd be in a better place. You believe the lie that you have to get the right degrees or the best grades or maybe sign up for a training program from the right inspirational speaker to make money.

- **No time.** You feel so overwhelmed by your job that all you can do is plop on the couch for a few minutes before you go to bed, wake up, and do it all over again the next day. You believe the lie that there's no extra time to make more money because you already work so much and come home to cook, clean, work out, and be with your family.

- **Lack of focus.** You have tons of amazing ideas for making money but no clue how to pick one and make it happen. So you keep yourself stuck in a cycle of coming up with a great idea, getting excited about it, talking about it, jotting down some notes, and moving along with your day. Rinse and repeat. You believe the lie that the most money comes to those with the most ideas.

- **No resources.** If it takes money to make money, you're already at a loss because you don't have any investors. And even if you did, you don't have a team to help you get started. There are too many people you'd need to hire to get things off the ground, and you have no way to pay them. You don't expect anyone to work for free, so you try to save some money to finally have enough to launch your idea. You believe the lie that your path to wealth must run through other people's property.

- **Fear of the unknown.** This is where your brain jumps into "what if" mode. *What if I fail? What if people judge me? What if I can't manage wealth? What if I pick a high-paying career and hate it?* You have no frame of reference for what you want to do, so you come up with all the reasons why it would be better to stay in your nice, familiar comfort zone. You believe the lie that by imagining the worst-case scenario about money, you can prevent trouble from coming your way.

- **Lack of self-worth.** You simply don't believe in yourself, and some part of you doesn't believe you're worthy of making more than you are at this moment. You're insecure, afraid, and uncertain about what will happen next. You make a lot of stupid mistakes you aren't proud of, and then you shame yourself into thinking you're not capable of making the changes necessary to get yourself out of your current situation. You believe the lie that you don't deserve money.

- **Thinking money is bad.** You've learned that if you want money, you're greedy. Since you believe that money is bad, you must be bad too for wanting more of it. Guilt and shame start rushing in, and you try to forget about the things you want to do by pushing those ideas away whenever they pop up in your head. You believe the lie that you won't be a good person anymore if you have a lot of money.

- **Self-sabotage.** When you have money, it becomes a burden and puts a strain on your life that you don't want. Maybe you have others asking you for financial support. Maybe you feel guilty for not helping more. Because you feel like that, you tend to spend your money too fast or give too much away and end up back where you started. You believe the lie that more money must come with more problems.

- **Lack of connections.** Having the "right" connections can help you make similar connections, and then you'll be on your way. But maybe you've never known anyone with money. And you feel weird about trying to make connections with people you don't already know. You believe the lie that the only way you can be rich is by having rich friends.

Do any of the points on that list resonate with you? Take a second to identify your top three. Remember, this is not a judgment on your current situation but a step toward understanding your struggles better. As we move forward, we'll explore these points further. For now, consciously becoming aware of them is a good starting point.

To be completely transparent, I've personally had to work through each and every item on that list. But let's not call them *excuses*. Let's call them what they really are: *stories*. That's exactly what they are—nothing more, nothing less. These stories may or may not align with reality, but know this:

Your Money Story is true for you and shapes everything you do.

Your Money
Story is
true for you
and shapes
everything
you do.

— Lewis Howes

If the story you tell yourself is that you have no time to make more money, why would you ever try to make the time to do it? If the story you tell yourself is that you are not worthy of wealth, why would you ever try to get any? If the story you tell yourself is that money is bad, why would you ever want more of it? And if you think you have no connections, why would you ever reach out to anyone? The reality is that our money struggles have little to do with money itself and everything to do with the stories we tell ourselves about it.

WE'VE ALL GOT THEM

Just work hard and you'll make money. How many times in your life did someone tell you that Money Story? How often did you tell yourself that if you weren't so lazy, you'd be a lot wealthier? Where did you learn that being successful meant always feeling exhausted and worn out? And how many times did you work really *hard* to make money only to realize it wasn't working?

That is exactly what happened to one writer and coach I know. She was 40 years old, living in a rented garage and driving a busted-up car. As a freelance writer, she had no doubt that she worked hard to make money. At one point she even knitted little things to sell her way of living as a "starving artist." When she finally looked at how hard she was hustling to get work by sending out emails, scheduling calls, closing on those calls, and then sitting down at her keyboard to complete a quality project for a client, she realized she was making a whopping sum—under a dollar an hour!

As a former rock band member, she told herself she'd be a "sell-out" if she made a lot of money with her writing. After all, having a creative path in life was supposed to bring some struggle and strife.

But she was sick and tired of living a struggling, broke life. So she read what felt like millions of self-help books that talked about the way your thoughts and beliefs shape your reality and began looking at the stories she told herself: *I can't make money as a writer. Money is bad. Rich people are gross.* And then it hit her—**if she could believe those negative things, why couldn't she choose to believe awesome things instead?**

At that point she decided to take more responsibility for her thoughts, beliefs, words, and actions. She told herself she didn't care how much proof to the contrary she had collected over the years. Her family members could make fun of her if they wanted to. It no longer mattered if she still had remnants of those old Money Stories. She was going to let herself feel excited about living a rich life and do whatever it took to reach her goal of making a real living as an entrepreneur.

She hired a coach who inspired her. Instead of giving in to the thought that it would be an irresponsible and impossible investment to hire a coach, she chose to go all in. She invested in herself and followed through with all her coach's suggestions and action steps—no matter how terrifying they felt.

Now Jen Sincero, the once-starving artist, coaches people all over the world, helping them transform their personal and professional lives. She has helped millions more with her books, including her first number-one *New York Times* bestseller, *You Are a Badass*, which has sold *millions of copies.* And it all started when she made the conscious decision to take a deep dive into understanding and changing her beliefs around money.

It's so easy for us to live with our Money Stories on autopilot. If we never take the time to ask ourselves about our own Money Stories and why we believe the things we do, we'll never have the opportunity to change. But your opportunity begins right now.

YOUR MONEY STORY

If you're ready to make money easy, I suggest you start by becoming more self-aware of your own Money Story. As you watch money move in and out of your life, I challenge you to start asking yourself why you do what you do with it.

Remember that being financially free isn't about how much money you make or how much is in your bank account. There are multimillionaires and billionaires with seemingly unlimited amounts of money who suffer inside and live lonely lives of misery. Being financially free is a state of being and has everything to do with the relationship you have with money and with your own self-worth.

To change the trajectory of your relationship and move closer to a life of financial peace and abundance, it's time to have a heart-to-heart with money. You may not understand all of why you do what you do right now, and that's all right. Just give yourself some time to become an observer. Without adding any judgment, guilt, or shame to your observations, answer these seven Money Story questions to see your current relationship for what it is:

1. **What did you learn about money as a child?** Reflecting on your childhood experiences can help you see where different feelings, beliefs, and behaviors about money originated. How did your parents, guardians, siblings, and friends talk about money? How did they experience wealth or the lack of it? When you can reflect on what influenced your relationship with money, it's easier to make conscious changes to the way you interact with and feel about money.

2. **What is your current relationship with money?** Try to be as open and honest with yourself as possible. How do you feel about money right now? Are you stressed, angry, thrilled, or excited? Is there another word that comes to mind? What are the habits you've picked up over time?

3. **What do you believe to be true about money?** Your beliefs about money drive your behaviors with money. Is money good, bad, or neither? Is it a tool? Is it a measure of success? Is it a status symbol? Or something else? Is it something only certain people can obtain, or is there enough for everyone? Once you can identify your beliefs about money, you can start to sort through which of your ideas are true and which are lies.

4. **How do your emotions affect your spending or saving?** When your feelings affect your financial decisions, you may not fully understand why you're

buying things. Are you going shopping or browsing online when you feel stressed, happy, or bored? Or are you constantly checking your bank balances for fear of missing something? Where do you think that behavior is coming from?

5. **What are your greatest financial fears?** Fear fuels action, so what you fear the most about money will determine what you do with money. Are you concerned about your debt? Are you afraid you might not be able to retire when you want? Remember, this is a time for reflection and not blaming or shaming yourself. It's important to know the fears you're living with so you can address them and eventually free yourself from the hold they have on you.

6. **What words do you use to talk about money?** Your language reveals your mindset. Do you use words like *lucky, discount, borrow, loan,* or *bills?* What about words like *invest, save, raise, affluent, entrepreneur,* or *prosperous?*

7. **How would you like your relationship with money to change?** It's always easier to move toward a target when you understand where you want to go. What does your ideal relationship with money look like? What would make you feel financially fulfilled and at peace with money? This vision of a different kind of relationship can help you stay motivated and keep you moving forward.

The more you do the work to understand your thoughts, feelings, and behaviors as they relate to money, the more opportunities you have for your Money Story to evolve and grow.

Now that you have a stronger understanding of your Money Story, I invite you to pause and think about one more question because it will shape your direction on this money journey:

What does being rich mean to you?

Back when I was trying to pay off my college debt, I read Ramit Sethi's *New York Times* best-selling book *I Will Teach You to Be Rich*. In his Netflix series, *How to Get Rich*, Ramit sits down with people to take an honest look at their finances and help them move closer to the rich life they envision. Ramit asks each client to define their rich life; then, they work on closing the gap between the client's current financial situation and where they want to be.

I find it fascinating that some couples on the show have similar visions of a rich life. Others hold drastically different ideas. One husband-to-be calls his fiancée a dreamer and surprises himself when he tells Ramit he sees himself as the dream crusher. Another man wants to have enough money so his mother, who worked so hard to take care of him, will be able to retire. A different couple first says they want to retire early but end up taking a monthlong vacation with their children.

No matter how they define their rich life, Ramit gives them a shared-story visualization exercise that offers them something to work toward. Focusing on what they really want helps them stop focusing on what they don't want, which could be anything from debt to impulse shopping. If they could have fixed their financial situation without Ramit's help, they would have done it. But without a concrete plan to work toward and someone to help them acknowledge and address their thoughts, feelings, and behaviors around money, it was too easy for them to simply keep the bills in an unopened stack and feel like they couldn't even dream about living a truly rich life.

Now it's your turn. You've given some thought to what your story has been, but now I invite you to dream about what it could become. Instead of giving up and giving in, it's time to make different choices. Your Money Story creates the context in which your unique natural Money Style can either flourish or diminish.

YOUR GAME PLAN

Exercise 1: Flip the Lie

In this chapter, we looked at the biggest challenges people say they face when it comes to money. You may believe some of these yourself, but can I be honest with you? These stories are actually lies you are telling yourself, and these lies keep you from money. The only way to combat a lie is to flip the script and replace it with truth. That's the goal of this exercise.

Under each of the headings that follow, you're going to write two statements. The first is the lie you believe about that challenge. The second is a truth that negates the lie. For example, for *no time* you may say, "I'd love to be able to create something that helps me earn extra money, but between my full-time job and my commute and taking care of my family, I don't have time." But when you stop to assess that statement, you realize that you spend at least three hours a day scrolling social media and binge-watching streaming shows. Armed with this new perspective, you might write this truth: "I have the same amount of time as everyone else, and if I use it more intentionally, I could find extra time to earn more money."

Make sense? Now it's your turn:

No training

Lie: _____

Truth:_____

No time

Lie: _____

Truth:_____

Lack of focus

Lie: _____

Truth:_____

No resources

Lie: _____

Truth: _____

Fear of the unknown

Lie: _____

Truth: _____

Negative self-worth

Lie: _____

Truth: _____

Money is bad

Lie: _____

Truth: _____

Self-sabotage

Lie: _____

Truth: _____

Lack of connections

Lie: _____

Truth: _____

Congratulations! If you've taken the time to work through these lies and flip the script, start to feel empowered. You are on your way to rewriting your Money Story.

Exercise 2: Define "Rich"

As you've seen from the stories we've discussed, and probably from people you've encountered in your own life, there are many and varied definitions of "rich." Most of these definitions have little to do with money. To truly make money easy, you have to know where it fits within your personal definition of rich.

In this exercise, you're going to brainstorm a list of things that make you feel rich and turn them into statements. It may be a great dinner with friends or traveling to new places or hanging out with family or mastering a new hobby. It might be writing a book or negotiating for yourself or deciding to change the way you see yourself. It might be a lot of money in the bank or just enough to pay the bills. It might be a beach house, or it might be #vanlife. It doesn't matter what your definition of rich is; what matters is that you articulate it and investigate it. By understanding your personal definition of richness, you can start to focus on the experiences that lead to a new Money Story—one in which every day is a rich day.

All you have to do is fill in the blank with whatever comes to mind—no matter how small or large it may seem.

I feel rich when _____

_____

_____

_____

_____

_____

Example: *I feel rich when I get to play a new song on my guitar for my girlfriend. I feel rich when I get a new stamp in my passport. I feel rich when I text an old friend and tell them how much they mean to me.*

Exercise 3: Reflect Every Night

To strengthen your money-beliefs muscles, start a reflection journal to help you bring lies about money to light so you can deal with them objectively and create a new Money Story. Without judgment, shame, or guilt, ask yourself a few questions as you wind down for the night.

- How were my thoughts and feelings today?
- Where did most of my money-based thoughts and feelings land today?
- When my thoughts and feelings were negative, how did I respond?
- What is one lesson I've learned about myself and my relationship with money today?

No matter the answers, you are learning and growing. As you create this nightly reflection habit, you'll see areas of strength and patterns that will help you understand areas for growth. Bringing your subconscious feelings and thoughts to your awareness is a pretty huge step toward creating a richer, more abundant life.

CHAPTER THREE

YOUR MONEY STYLE

Quick question: Which one are you: spender, saver, shopper, hoarder, or investor? Has anyone else ever told you that you were one of these? I see a lot of online quizzes designed to squeeze you into one of these or similar boxes. Maybe you've even told others that's who you are, as if your approach to money is somehow a fixed part of your identity.

But what if I told you that when it comes to your relationship with money, names like *saver* or *spender* are just labels put on you? They are not a reflection of who you are or who you have to be. Do you find that idea freeing? Exciting? Maybe even slightly scary?

Yes, it's true that you have natural behavioral tendencies hardwired into your personality. Just as some people are naturally more introverted or extroverted, you may be wired to spend, save, or invest your money. These natural tendencies make up what I call your Money Style. But those organic Money Styles then get shaped by your Money Story—that is, by what has happened *to* and *with* you.

It may help to think of it this way: Your Money Style is the result of your built-in tendencies. You didn't choose them; you were just born with them. To be sure, influences in your environment have shaped who you are and even caused wounds that affect how you avoid painful parts of your Money Story. But certain things are simply part of your behavioral DNA, if you will. Your Money Style is the result of the choices you have made and of your responses to the actions and inputs of others.

However, the labels that get slapped on you by yourself or others are often more the result of how your story has shaped your style than a product of who you are or must be. At the end of the day, neither your style nor your story determines your future strategy when it comes to money. But once you become aware of your style and story, you can decide for yourself what you want to change to create your Money Strategy. I call it the Money Strategy Formula, and it looks like this:

Style x Story = Strategy

Your natural Money Style multiplied by your Money Story gets you to one side of the equation—but you can understand your style and choose the direction of your story as you move forward. You can change your story to craft the strategy that gets you to a place where you are living a richer life.

You are not merely the product of your style and story. You *can* change. And when you do, you can decide for yourself what your Money Strategy will be as part of who you choose to become.

Let's break down the Money Strategy Formula, starting with the first component: your Money Style. Each of us comes into this world with certain behavioral tendencies. As you grow up, those tendencies get shaped by a million little influences and emotions tied to money experiences and repeated over and over again. You watch other people respond to money. Listen to teachings about money. Believe certain creeds about money. You may even develop learned behaviors over time as you figure out how best to interact with other people around money. These behaviors function a lot like default settings, so they can often come out when you feel under pressure, afraid, or anxious.

Neither your
style nor
your story
determines
your future
strategy.

— Lewis Howes

I've created a simple assessment tool to help you uncover your natural Money Style. Keep in mind that we're not trying to psychoanalyze you or do a deep psychological profile, nor is this tool intended to provide financial advice. We're painting with a broad brush here to identify significant tendencies based on your behavioral DNA. It is also important to note that no one style is better than another, and each style comes with unique natural benefits and potential barriers.

Let's take a few minutes to discover which of the four Money Styles is most likely your own. As you read each of the following scenarios, choose the response you would most likely tend to have. Some of the scenarios clearly connect to money while others assess how you respond to life inputs in general to get a sense of your natural wiring in certain situations. There are no right or wrong responses, so don't overthink it.

1. Your cousin lets you know he has a "can't miss" investment opportunity.

Your most likely response:

A. Tell him to show you the numbers. If it makes sense, let's do it!

B. You're excited about the possibilities and can't wait to dive in. You'll work it out as you go.

C. Applaud your cousin for pursuing his dream. You want to encourage him but also take a closer look at the situation to make sure it doesn't harm your relationship.

D. You ask to see his business plan and the numbers behind it. You want to know if he's done his homework before you do research of your own.

2. Congratulations! You had an unexpected windfall of money come your way.

Your most likely response:

A. Supercharge your dream of starting a business and becoming your own CEO!

B. It's time to celebrate, travel the world, and create memorable adventures with family and friends.

C. You check in with your close family and friends to see if anyone has a need.

D. You put the money in a safe bank account while you analyze your current budget and make a plan for how to best use it.

3. You saved some money and are ready to make some investments, so you reached out to a financial advisor who wants to review your financial situation.

Your most likely response:

A. You prepare questions that will challenge her to consider new investments that will help your assets grow even more than she could plan.

B. You feel a little stressed about the conversation since you don't feel you have a firm grasp on the details—but you really enjoy talking with her!

C. You welcome an opportunity to secure your family's financial future. Before meeting, you check in with your key people to hear any needs or concerns.

D. You thoroughly prepare for the review by checking all the numbers and analyzing the data you've personally gathered.

4. Your friends suggest a hangout this weekend via a group text and are open to ideas.

Your most likely response:

A. "I know a great place to eat and can get us reservations. Plus, there's a show at a nearby theater with good reviews. I can get us tickets for it in advance."

B. "I'm in! We can explore the downtown area and pick a place that feels like what we want. Maybe a show after dinner or something fun. We'll figure it out!"

C. "What type of restaurants would everyone prefer? Are there any shows you've been wanting to see? I'm down for whatever the group decides!"

D. "What's our price range for dinner? It's a Saturday night, so we might want to consider reservations and the parking situation if we decide to go downtown. I'll look into some options."

5. You just found a 30-day challenge online to cut spending and increase savings.

Your most likely response:

A. You love the challenge but figure you can accelerate the plan and get the same results in only 15 days.

B. It sounds cool and just might work, so you figure, *Why not? I'll give it a shot!*

C. You share the link with a few friends to see if they will join you in doing the challenge together.

D. You look up the challenge online to see if it's legit, to determine what it entails, and to check for any reviews before you commit to it.

6. **You finally found the perfect place to live, but it costs a little more than you had planned.**

Your most likely response:

A. You know it's what you want, so you'll find a way to make it happen.

B. You go for it because you believe that when you follow your dreams, good things happen. If it's meant to be, it will work out.

C. You talk about it with friends you trust and anyone who might be living with you. If it works for them, you might be willing to go for it, but you want to be sure.

D. If you can figure out how to rework your budget, you just might go for it. Otherwise, you may pass on this one.

7. **As you wait in line at the checkout, your favorite snack starts calling your name.**

Your most likely response:

A. You need energy to get stuff done, so it's a no-brainer. You grab it and go.

B. It would brighten up your day and give you the energy you need for a fun morning, so why not?

C. You're hesitant to grab one since it wasn't on your initial list, but you remember you had also been planning to pick up something to share at work. Perfect! You can get the share size and let your colleagues enjoy it too.

D. You check your budget app, as well as the calories, to see if you can afford it. If so, you'll love it. If not, you'll leave it.

8. **While checking out at your favorite online retailer, you see a suggested purchase that looks cool and doesn't cost that much extra to add to your order.**

    Your most likely response:

    A. You don't waste time making the decision. Just add it. You're confident you'll find a way to work it into the budget later.

    B. You love the suggestion and add it to your cart. What luck! You just upgraded your day!

    C. You hadn't planned on getting anything else and should probably consider the trade-offs before deciding. If you buy this now, it may mean you can't get something else you need later. You bookmark it and stick to your current order.

    D. You need to research more about that item. It looks good, but why does it cost so little? Is there a problem with it? It's probably best to think about it and come back later.

9. **A family member is asking for financial help for the third time this year.**

    Your most likely response:

    A. You give them a firm no. Giving them money isn't working. They need to make better decisions.

    B. You give them what money you have available because you see their potential and feel it in your gut that this time could be different.

    C. You take the time to listen to their problems and offer to try to find more resources to help them. Even if you have doubts, you'll likely give something just to preserve the relationship.

D. You offer to help them evaluate their financial plans and even invest in a course to teach them good practices, but you'll only give them cash if you see a clear path to better results.

10. You want to leave a business venture with a long-time friend who has lost money, but they ask for one last conversation to convince you to stay.

Your most likely response:

A. You know what you want, so you candidly explain why you're leaving, focusing on the facts to clearly explain why it's best for you to move on.

B. You listen to what they have to say, but if your gut is still telling you not to stay, you won't. Even if this venture isn't the one, odds are you'll find a good one soon.

C. These conversations are always uncomfortable for you, and when they start to cry, you wonder if leaving is the right thing to do, regardless of the numbers.

D. You listen to their case and note the evidence for both options. You want to be sure you haven't missed something before making an informed decision.

Now simply add up your scores for each letter option A–D.

A _____ **B** _____ **C** _____ **D**_____

If you answered mostly A's, your money style is **The Director.**
If you answered mostly B's, your money style is **The Energizer.**
If you answered mostly C's, your money style is **The Shepherd.**
If you answered mostly D's, your money style is **The Analyzer.**

My Money Style is

_____

If you have two styles that are tied, read the following descriptions to determine which one best describes your natural style. Now let's unpack each of the styles.

The Director. This style focuses on driving forward and crashing through barriers to get things done. Directors often like to try new things and challenge the status quo. They're all about growth and expansion, making things bigger and better. Directors not only think outside the box, they figure out how to blow up the box! Their drive to achieve is strong, so financial goals are often naturally front and center.

BENEFITS OF A DIRECTOR	THINGS DIRECTORS COMMONLY SAY
Self-starter	*What are we waiting for?*
Focused on results	*Show me the money!*
Favors facts over feelings	*Show me the facts.*
Not intimidated by challenges	*We can do this!*
Willing to make the tough decisions	*This isn't working. We need to pivot.*
Cool under pressure	*No need to panic. I've got this.*
Has a strong action bias	*Let's get busy!*

The Energizer. This style is enthusiastic about, well, almost everything. They love engaging with people, and others often see them as the life of the party. But Energizers generally don't like the rigid feeling they get from detailed planning. They'd much rather make it up as they go and trust that the universe will have their back when it comes to financial needs.

BENEFITS OF AN ENERGIZER	THINGS ENERGIZERS COMMONLY SAY
Brings the energy	*I'm excited about the possibilities!*
Keeps an optimistic outlook	*When one door closes, another opens.*
Likes options and opportunities	*There are a lot of things we could do.*
Often has great financial instincts	*My gut tells me we should . . .*
Thrives on being spontaneous	*No plan? No problem.*
Comfortable with big ideas	*Let's dream a little, shall we?*

The Shepherd. This style is all about getting along and helping everyone else get along. Shepherds thrive on creating warm, welcoming, and accepting environments. They tend to make financial decisions by asking, *How will this decision help or harm other people? Will everyone be okay if I make this or that move?*

BENEFITS OF A SHEPHERD

Good at following
the plan

Moves slowly into new things

Keeps focus on one
thing at a time

Sees the practical impact

Helps ease
financial tensions

Favors feelings
over facts

Patient, willing to wait

THINGS SHEPHERDS COMMONLY SAY

*Just stick with
what we planned.*

Let's not rush into this.

Don't get distracted.

How will this affect that?

*No need to get upset.
Let's work together.*

*Does this feel right
for everyone?*

Think long-term.

The Analyzer. This style loves order and method and tends to think of themselves as more introverted. Analyzers like to analyze financial decisions every which way before actually choosing a course of action. They like to really dive in to discover all the facts before making a money move. Analyzers tend to think, *If I can just understand all the details and create an incredible financial plan, all my money struggles will be over.*

BENEFITS OF AN ANALYZER	THINGS ANALYZERS COMMONLY SAY
Good at getting tasks done	*What's next on the list?*
Realistic and practical	*How is this going to work?*
Pushes through challenges	*I don't know what quit means.*
Candid	*I don't think that will work because . . .*
Always has a plan and a schedule	*Right place. Right time. Right results.*
Gets the details right	*Is that accurate or is it just a ballpark?*
Sets up helpful systems	*Why think about it? Automate it.*

Keep in mind that these styles are not intended to be rigid boxes. No one completely fits within one style because each person is unique. But in general, you will have one dominant style as your default setting. And you may have two styles that you think are each naturally part of your makeup.

SHADOW STYLES

When you identify your natural Money Style tendencies, you can better understand why you tend to respond to money the way you do. But it is also important to know that all Money Styles have a potential dark side. I call them Shadow Styles.

If you think of your natural Money Style as the hero, then these Shadow Styles are the villains, turning the benefits that can come from your strengths into barriers to your success. When you overplay your natural style with money, without concern for the important things in life, your style can cast a very dark shadow.

The Director becomes *the Dictator.* The drive to achieve more—always more—can leave a wake of broken relationships, mental trauma, or unhealthy physical stress. The shadow often begins creeping in slowly, around the edges of life, as the drive to achieve goals seems to outweigh the "sacrifices" needed to get there.

WEAKNESSES OF A DICTATOR	THINGS DICTATORS COMMONLY SAY
Doesn't value input	*No one asked what you think.*
Avoids helpful routines and details	*I can't be bothered to check that.*
Struggles to think of others	*It works for me, so I guess it's good.*
Overcommits self and others	*Yes, we can do it by then!*
Sacrifices healthy practices	*I'm too busy to work out today.*
Doesn't want to wait	*I should have had a return by now.*
Expresses discontent or appears uncaring	*Is that the best you can do?*

The Energizer becomes *the Eccentric*. The need to feel spontaneous can leave someone with no clear plan. Instead they end up just winging it all the time and depending on other people to bail them out when they get into financial trouble. Sure, they can be the life of the party, but when overdone, this style can be draining or a burden on other people.

WEAKNESSES OF AN ECCENTRIC

Feels the need to get approval

Tends to be overly optimistic

Lacks focus and organization

Gets emotional under stress

Needs help after winging it doesn't work

Ignores rules and procedures

Unprepared but overconfident

THINGS ECCENTRICS COMMONLY SAY

Yes, but do you like it?

I'm sure it will all work out somehow.

When was I supposed to file that?

Money stuff always makes me so upset!

Oops! Can I borrow money to cover that?

I figured we could just make it work.

Well, I thought I had it all figured out.

The Shepherd becomes *the Doormat*. The desire to keep everybody happy can destroy a Shepherd's zeal, erode their confidence, and cause their friendships to wither right in front of them. When overdone, this style can mean someone unintentionally lets other people walk all over their own financial health, ignores self-care, and eventually becomes bitter when they start to feel that their caring energy has gone unappreciated.

WEAKNESSES OF A DOORMAT	THINGS DOORMATS COMMONLY SAY
Hesitates to express their desires	*As long as it works for everyone else . . .*
Appears passive-aggressive	*Fine. I guess so. If that's what you want.*
Lacks a big-picture vision	*As long as I'm helping someone today . . .*
Dislikes confrontation about money	*Oh, I'd rather not have that conversation.*
Trusts people too easily	*I can't believe they would do that to me!*
Doesn't like making changes	*It's always worked just fine the way it is.*
Tends not to take action	*I'm sure something will come up.*

The Analyzer becomes *the Perfectionist*. The hunger to get everything just right can become debilitating when overdone. This style can tend to fixate on financial details and bank balances, hoarding more "just in case" something might go wrong. It can lead to simply sucking all the joy out of life and leaving people stuck with money but no sense of peace or freedom.

WEAKNESSES OF A PERFECTIONIST

THINGS PERFECTIONISTS COMMONLY SAY

WEAKNESSES OF A PERFECTIONIST	THINGS PERFECTIONISTS COMMONLY SAY
Tends to think worst case	*This probably will not work.*
Appears secluded or secretive	*Why do I need to share that info?*
Can come across as inflexible	*Why should I have to change my plan?*
Depends on rules too much	*Just tell me the right way to do it.*
Lacks confidence despite being prepared	*I don't know. . . am I ready for that?*
Focuses on getting it perfect	*I won't invest until . . .*
Gets lost in the weeds	*Let me check that—for the tenth time . . .*

These Shadow Styles can be challenging because they feel so "right" to each of us as we lean in to what we are naturally wired to do. But when we ignore their impact on other important factors in life, we set ourselves up for a life of lack and stress rather than a life of fulfillment and peace.

THE MULTIPLYING FACTOR

Once you identify your Money Style, you can then understand how the second part of the formula shapes it. Remember that your Money Story is the sum of all that has happened to you that affects how you think and act when it comes to money. It also includes what you have done to this point: the thoughts, beliefs, and scripts regarding money that you have let live within you.

However, your story serves as a catalyst of sorts, a multiplying factor that shapes how you express your style, usually in one of the following three ways:

1. **It aligns.** This happens when your natural style is free to be clearly expressed and is encouraged to grow in all its benefits. Basically, when your life experience lines up exactly with your natural style, life is good. Truth be told, though, it's rare for this to happen completely; it can easily happen in some areas and not others. For example, if you had a parent or grandparent who taught you about your relationship with money, you might find that part of your story in greater alignment than other parts.

2. **It amplifies.** This happens when your Shadow Style kicks in. Circumstances may have reinforced the value of your strengths to the point where you unintentionally overplay your benefits in an unhealthy way. For example, over time, you may have learned that just winging it has worked for you. So you make it your go-to move, and your relationship with money goes off course.

3. **It diminishes and distorts.** This happens when, for any number of reasons, your story causes you to suppress your natural benefits and focus on barriers. For example, perhaps your parents pushed back on your desire to drive forward and achieve goals. Instead, they encouraged you to focus on getting aligned with others. Both have their place, of course, but by

unintentionally diminishing your style, you leave your best on the table of life. And it causes your relationship with money to feel suppressed as you struggle to make sense of it from a place of weakness rather than a place of strength.

This is why it is worth diving deeper into understanding your Money Story—so you can see how it has shaped the way you express your natural Money Style. Once you are aware, you can empower yourself to do something about it going forward.

Katy Milkman is a professor at the Wharton School of the University of Pennsylvania, host of the behavioral economics podcast *Choiceology*, and author of *How to Change: The Science of Getting from Where You Are to Where You Want to Be.* I know making lasting changes to your Money Story isn't easy, and that's why I asked Katy, "What is the number-one thing we need to know about changing our behavior for the better?"

Here is what she told me: "Trying to figure out, 'What are the barriers for you?' And matching the tools that you put together to build your strategy to help with what's holding you back."[1]

By now you may have begun to get a sense of what those barriers might be for you, the challenges your story presents to expressing your style through a clear Money Strategy. To help you heal those barriers, it's time to dive deeper into your relationship with money by taking yourself to money therapy. Book a time with a financial coach, attend a money class, or research online to explore free resources. These are some ways you can develop those "matching tools" Katy speaks of to build an effective approach for future financial success.

I know change is possible. What has happened to you in the past does not necessarily determine what is possible in the future. Whatever labels have been put on you in the past when it comes to money—irresponsible, tightwad, greedy, big spender, saver, hoarder—you can peel them off and create a new Money Strategy that better aligns with who you want to become.

But here's the key: you need to take ownership of your mindset to begin your money reset.

You can create
a new Money
Strategy that
better aligns
with who you
want to become.

— Lewis Howes

YOUR GAME PLAN

If you haven't completed the Money Styles assessment (page 38), do so now. If you want to go deeper, try this exercise:

Exercise 1: Sequencing Your Money DNA ($DNA)

In your physical body, your DNA carries the genetic instructions for your growth and development. Its double-helix structure serves as a scaffold that makes it stable. In the same way, your $DNA is the stable scaffold that carries instructions for how you can make and grow your money.

Your $DNA begins with your **experiences** and **influences**. In turn, your experiences and influences determine your **emotions** about money. For example, my **experience** of stealing money from my dad's client created the first strand. My dad's anger about that experience **influenced** my view of money—the other strand of my $DNA. Each strand was linked together by my **feelings** about the incident: my humiliation, anger, and powerlessness.

What does your $DNA look like? Take a moment to reflect on some of the experiences that led to your Money Story. Write about how each experience has influenced you. Then articulate what feelings have been created. When you understand how these three things connect, you can begin to "resequence" your $DNA and write a new story.

Experience: _____

Emotional story you tell yourself about it:

_____

_____

_____

Experience: _____

Emotional story you tell yourself about it:

_____

_____

_____

Experience: _____

Emotional story you tell yourself about it:

_____

_____

_____

Experience: _____

Emotional story you tell yourself about it:

_____

_____

_____

Experience: _____

Emotional story you tell yourself about it:

_____

_____

_____

STEP 2

Reset Your Money Mindset

Now that you've discovered a lot about your money story, style, and the power you have to change your strategy, it's time to hit the Reset button with money. You need to first look back and begin healing your relationship with money, then look forward to see how money aligns with your Meaningful Mission. When you combine both perspectives, you're ready to reset your money mindset. That's Step 2, where you begin to lay the foundation for a new and improved relationship with money. Keep in mind that everyone's story is unique, so your story and results will be different from mine. I share this to inspire, inform, and empower you on your journey, not to give you specific financial advice. With that being said, let's get started to reset your mindset!

Find more free resources to accelerate your growth and make money easy at MakeMoneyEasyBook.com.

CHAPTER FOUR

HEAL YOUR
RELATIONSHIP
WITH MONEY

Back in the days when kids could still buy candy with coins, two eight-year-old twin boys each received a quarter from their father. As they walked down the street toward the local store, thinking about what they would buy with that shiny quarter, one twin kept his quarter safely tucked away in his pocket. The other happily walked along, flipping his quarter into the air and smiling to himself every time he caught it.

Until he didn't. When the quarter flipped beyond his reach, he watched in frantic horror as it dropped through the sewer drain at the side of the road. He immediately threw himself onto the grate, stretching his arm through the narrow opening as far as it would go. When his arm couldn't quite reach the bottom to retrieve his quarter, he felt his stomach tighten and became sickened with disappointment. When his brother came out of the store chewing his newly purchased bubble gum, he began to cry and headed home empty-handed.

When they got home, their dad met them outside and noticed he wasn't chewing gum and asked, "So what did you get?"

His son avoided eye contact as he felt fresh tears welling up. "Papa, I lost my quarter."

"What do you mean you lost it?" His father's tone said more than his words.

"Well, I was flipping it and . . ." The boy choked on the rest of his story.

"Never play with your money!" his father erupted. The boy could feel the tears running down his cheeks again as his father stomped back into the house, leaving him feeling quite alone outside.

The boy noticed that his grandfather had observed the exchange, so he walked over to him, hoping for some advice. His grandfather put an arm around his shoulder and said, "Your papa has a point about not playing with money. But there's another way to look at this." The boy sniffed and turned his face toward his grandfather, who continued with a wink, "Never go anywhere with just one quarter to lose."

That young boy was Grant Cardone, who told me he remembers that day like it was yesterday. He still believes money isn't something we should play with, and if you've ever heard him talk about money, you know he takes it very seriously. But he also still agrees with his grandfather—it's always better to have more money than you need.

Instead of living life being afraid to lose money, he has learned how to have a better relationship with it by learning to take care of it. Grant told me this:

> Money is secretive for most people . . . Most people don't know what they make because they want to keep it a secret. Drug addicts don't know how much they use. The alcoholic doesn't know how much they drink. They're not accounting for anything, and the relationship then goes bad. You've got to inventory your money. The first thing I look at every day is my money, so I have a great relationship with it.

Grant could have chosen to let that quarter experience scar his Money Story. He could have chosen to live in fear of losing money. Instead he chose to dive in and heal his relationship with money.

Agree with Grant or not, you can't argue with his success. Today he's a real estate investor with billions under his management, an equity fund manager, and co-founder or investor in nearly 20 businesses. And the same choice Grant made is available to you.

Whether you know it or not, you have a relationship with money. As we've seen, that relationship has been shaped by your Money Story. We learn how to create a relationship with money in the same way we figured out how to interact with other people when we were children—observation and experience. Our minds interpret what we noticed about our parents, older family members, and others we encountered as they interacted with money. It's tough to try to repair a relationship with another person, let alone with something as complicated as money. But the longer you ignore the fact that your relationship with money could use some improvements, the worse it gets. Jay Shetty, best-selling author and podcast host of *On Purpose*, says it perfectly: "By feeling uncomfortable to address money, you spend more time obsessed with the lack of it."[1]

And until you heal your relationship with money, nothing can change for the better. Because if you don't care for your money, your money won't care for you.

MY RELATIONSHIP WITH MONEY

When I was growing up, I was constantly reminded that while we had a home to live in, I went to public school and money didn't "grow on trees." And it started early, around something almost every young boy wants to play: video games.

One day, I went home and asked my parents for a Nintendo. I'd been hearing the kids at school and at the arcade excitedly discuss their gaming exploits, and I wanted to be one of the group. My parents quickly and clearly let me know we didn't have the money for such things. They had been saying the same thing for many years whenever I asked for the latest toy, and I could tell their word on the topic was final.

If you don't care
for your money,
your money won't
care for you.

— Lewis Howes

During summer days, neighborhood kids filled the church parking lot down the street. They turned over two giant blue recycling bins at each end to serve as goals for rollerblade hockey. We split into teams, and it was game on—only I didn't have rollerblades. Everyone else rolled around on wheels, chasing after the ball with their hockey sticks. And there I was, running around in my sneakers, using a borrowed, beat-up stick to score goals with everyone else. If I had waited until my parents could afford to buy me a pair of rollerblades, I never would have played.

Most of my childhood was like that. I seemed to always be just a little on the outside of things because we didn't have enough money. For example, when the cool kids started a club, I wanted in. At eight years old, I imagined myself as a member of the club, going to meetings in someone's basement, eating snacks, and playing Nintendo. But they didn't let just anyone in. There were only two ways to join the club: pass a test by answering a list of questions correctly or pay $5. I didn't have any money, so I opted for the test. Question #1: *Name someone who walked on the moon.* Uuumm . . . I had nothing. Question #2: *Name the first three presidents of the United States.* Washington and . . . uh . . . sigh. I remember feeling so stupid, but I had to try the only option I had left. I went home and asked Mom for the money.

She said she didn't have $5, but we scrounged around the house, looking under couch cushions and anywhere else we thought we might find a misplaced quarter. We tossed anything we found into an empty shoebox until I finally had enough. Even though my mom had found a way to make it happen, I felt a deep awareness of lacking money. Then a funny thing happened: I handed my money to the other two boys who started "the club." But I left the first meeting feeling humiliated. Not only was I not smart enough to join the club, I had to pay to have friends.

I later came to realize that the deeper message I took away from this experience wasn't just that I didn't have much money but that *I didn't have much value.*

All of these experiences shaped my relationship with money as a young adult. To me money was like a superhero friend that I really wanted in my life but was too powerful to be around. When I had money in my hands, I felt like I had a greater sense of control, a new power, and an ability to do something. And when I didn't have it, I wanted it back in my life, but I didn't know how to manage it and definitely did not understand it. My relationship with money was dangerous and shameful yet exciting and terrifying—all at the same time.

Early in my entrepreneurial endeavors, I used to overwork because I was terrified that I'd lose money. I'd save and work day and night. I always felt the pressure was on me emotionally and financially to make sure things kept running, as opposed to working in a career that had a definite start and stop to my days.

For many years, I was anxious about money because I didn't have it. Then when I had it, I was still anxious and didn't enjoy it as much as I could have, but I also didn't feel like I needed to buy things. My focus was on making sure there was enough money in the bank. And with every new chapter of life, I think I'll continue to heal my relationship with money in different ways as my finances continue to grow and change.

Not so long ago, I realized I was subconsciously on the lookout for people who were messing with my money. I'd get emotional, upset, and angry. Unfortunately, I sent some reactive messages into the world back then. I now know that my reactive behaviors came from my dad's anger when he caught me stealing, mixed with my feelings of being taken advantage of and abused as a child. I felt like people were stealing from me if they weren't delivering on the promises in our agreements. I still have some tendencies to want to react in a frustrated way when I feel like something isn't fair. But now that I've realized where the root of those kinds of reactions comes from, I can step back and observe the situation and consider my options before reacting.

It's still hard for me to accept someone buying me lunch or a coffee. I know that might sound pretty silly, but we're all works in progress. So many times when I lived with my sister, I felt guilty when people helped me out financially, and now that I have my own money, I don't like the feeling of relying on others to pay for anything. I allow people to do it sometimes now, but it's a constant practice of allowing and receiving because that's part of living a richer life—receiving a gift from another and not robbing them of that generous act. Either way, I'm making some progress because I am aware of why my relationship with money is the way it is.

Have you ever believed that if you lost money, you'd be broke on the streets? Maybe you grew up in an environment that was filled with scarcity. Maybe you didn't feel like you were important or valued in your relationships with your family and friends. You may have similar thoughts running through your mind:

- Am I enough for this relationship with or without money?
- Am I worthy of having money?
- Would anyone pay me money for what I can do?
- I'm too young to have money.
- I'm not experienced enough to have money.
- I'm not qualified to manage money.

No matter how many times you've thought these things, I need you to hear me. *You are worthy.* You are never too old or too young. Any kind of healing begins with taking responsibility for your behaviors, asking why you do the things you do, and acting on that kind of clarity. Experience, qualifications, and skills are things you can get once you're clear on your Meaningful Money Mission.

As many people have said in various ways, it's easier to behave yourself into a new way of thinking than to think yourself into a new way of acting. In other words, act first, and you'll start believing instead of waiting to believe before you take action.

MONEY TRAUMA

"Money trauma is the only trauma that we wake up and work for the rest of our lives." That's what Scott Donnell, founder of seven companies who has spent over a decade studying some of the wealthiest families in the world, told me. Every day, no matter what sorts of wounds we have related to money, we still have to deal with money. We can't avoid it or just stay away from it. We have to engage with it. And at the same time, our money trauma shapes how we approach it, so we end up working "for" it for the rest of our lives. At the end of the day, our money trauma can shape our sense of self-worth and self-confidence, and even our very identity, if we let it.

I was only about 10 years old when I experienced what proved to be some pretty serious money trauma. My dad had given me a little U.S. Postal Service piggy bank where I proudly stored every coin or dollar bill I got.

During the summer, one of my older sisters seemed to always have a bunch of teenage friends over to just hang out. I thought I would impress a few of the teen boys and show them the bank stashed under my bed in my bedroom and the cash I had saved inside of it. I felt pleased with myself until I checked the bank a few hours later—all the money was gone. I had been robbed. In my own bedroom.

And then I realized my mistake. The bank had a sticker on the bottom with a simple access code. I had unwittingly shown the gang exactly how to steal my money.

I stormed down the stairs. "Look, the money was in the bank, and then I showed it to you—and now it is gone." I expected a full confession and my money to be promptly returned. Instead, I got a chorus of, "We didn't take it." And that was that.

From this experience, my previous stealing spree, and other experiences, I learned what it felt like to have money taken from me and to take money from others. I came to know the deep disappointment I felt, both with how I felt about other people and what other people felt about me. As a result, I often felt tremendous guilt about my stealing behavior, even decades later as an adult.

A lot of money trauma happens when people and money are simply out of alignment with an agreement to exchange value. For example, if I'm just abusing the value of others by taking from them without an equal and consensual exchange, I am out of alignment—emotionally, spiritually, and psychologically—in that interaction. On the other hand, if I am giving money as a gift out of the kindness of my heart, I am in alignment because I am willingly sharing value.

As a child, when I stole money—or stole anything, really—I was out of alignment. I hadn't earned it and had no right to it. Being out of alignment created an emotional wound within me. The more I did it, the bigger the wound became, the stronger the story felt, and the harder it was to break that pattern of behavior. Once I had normalized it, or better yet, *justified* it, I thought I could get away with being out of alignment without consequences. It made me feel powerful in the moment to steal, although it was a truly disempowering action to take advantage of someone in that way.

This sense of being out of alignment can be about small things that you dismiss as nothing but over time build and become bigger wounds. Parents often unintentionally create these wounds with well-meaning statements: *We can't afford that. Do you have any idea how much that costs? Money doesn't grow on trees. Do you know how hard I worked to get you this, and you just broke it? What a waste!* And so on. They unintentionally cause children to develop a negative connotation around all things related to money.

You might also come to feel out of alignment if you believe you are doing a job or delivering a service but not getting paid what you're worth. As we'll unpack in the chapters to come, you can do something about that by using the Money Habits, but for now, just acknowledge that there are a lot of ways you have probably developed money wounds without even realizing it at the time.

Whether someone stole from you, took advantage of you and your money, manipulated you to get your money, or abused the relationship in a way that involved money, there's a trauma associated with that. And you have told yourself a story about it. Now, the story may be true, but if you allow that to be your story, you'll never heal your relationship with money. The wound will continue until you reclaim your power and heal from that wound.

It doesn't mean what happened to you was good, right, or even okay. But by learning how to heal from it, you give yourself more power in the future and minimize the emotional impact of it. You won't lose the memory, per se, but you won't have the same debilitating emotions tied to it.

Why do these wounds matter when it comes to making money easy? Because these wounds have an energy to them. A scientist might call this quantum physics. A religious person might call it prayer. An atheist might call it the placebo effect. A spiritual person might call it the Law of Attraction. Whatever it is, the energy connected with money wounds attracts similar energy to it. When you live in a painful energetic space with a lacking mindset, you attract more pain and lack. But when you heal your money wounds and live from a positive energetic space, you can open yourself up to attracting more positive abundance.

MAKE MONEY YOUR FRIEND

Now that I have been on a journey to heal my relationship with money, I don't feel the guilt I once did about letting people pay for me, and I enjoy paying for people too. I don't do it from a place of shame or guilt anymore but from a place of feeling abundant. I feel grateful for the value I am creating in life and want to give gifts to friends and family.

But if someone blocks a gift someone wants to give them, they are blocking an energy exchange. If they refuse the gift, it's like they are robbing that person of actually giving that gift. On the other hand, if they say nothing in return or they're not appreciative, that also blocks the giving energy, showing a lack of appreciation for the value I or anyone brings to the relationship.

I even think that when you receive money, it's a good practice to thank money. That's right. Say, "Thank you, money, for coming my way. And thank you to the person who gave it to me." In doing so, you'll create more energy flow to receive more. Likewise, when you have the ability to give someone money, you should say, "I'm so grateful that I have this money coming to me, so I can give more."

The energy
connected with
money wounds
attracts similar
energy to it.

— Lewis Howes

Ken Honda, international best-selling author of *Happy Money: The Japanese Art of Making Peace with Your Money*, suggests the same thing:

> When money comes, say *arigato* or "thank you" to money. And when you pay money, when money leaves your life, once again say *arigato* to your money. Really, thank the money for staying with you. Even if it was a short visit, thank it for staying. Money will love that.
>
> And then, at night, money will just start to say, "Ken is a good place to go." And then money will come back.[2]

Be open to feeling good about the energy flowing in both directions. If you're blocking it, you're saying, "No, I can't do this," and then you keep those opportunities from flowing to you. But if you feel emotionally good about it, you rewire yourself to create more of those situations.

According to Ken Honda, the key to healing your relationship with money is to become friends with it:

> My favorite question to ask people is: If money was a person, who would it be? Would it be a fun person, always joking and always entertaining you? Or is it somebody like an assassin who's going to try to hurt you or scare you? Or gangsters who try to intimidate you?
>
> If you are complaining, money may not be such a fun, good person. By complaining, you make money by being a villain, and you don't want that scary person living in your house.
>
> Just look at it from money's perspective. If you've been complaining about it, the feeling is mutual. If you complain about it, money will say, "No. I'm not going to come to you."[3]

This means honestly looking at how you feel about money and making the commitment to change your perspective so you can shift your emotions. Only then can you cultivate the right energy flow between you and money. If you don't want it near you, why would it come to you? But if you make it your friend, it feels welcome. I love Ken's perspective because it really takes us out of our egos and helps us see things from a broader perspective. When we realize that we have a relationship with money and that it's reciprocal, we can understand more clearly why we're having trouble with it.

Our relationship with money is an emotionally intense, intimate relationship. Even though it involves numbers, it isn't a typical analytical relationship. Our money wounds are often attached to memories and stories we tell ourselves about those memories. There is energy stored in each of those memories. Often we simply can't go back and undo or retrace our steps. But Joe Dispenza says that we don't necessarily need to resolve the wound. What we can do is heal the memory of the wound by finding a new way to retell the story associated with it.

I should note that these moments in our past can traumatize us in small or big ways, but they can also motivate us to become greater—to take action, develop value, learn new skills, get uncomfortable, and push past our fears. In other words, we are not helpless victims of our stories.

For example, when my dad was injured in that car accident, I no longer had his financial support to fall back on. It was traumatic, to be sure, but it also moved me to take ownership of my own financial future. In the same way, when I was picked last for dodgeball in fourth grade, it pushed me to want to get better at sports so I wouldn't be the last one picked. That drive eventually landed me in professional football and on the USA Team Handball national team. It's not our wounds that matter; it's how we interpret the memory of the wound and how we respond to it that matters.

Our goal in healing these wounds is to be driven not by anger, resentment, or shame but by a desire to learn to accept and forgive ourselves for where we are and for the things we didn't know. Then we can build from a place of pursuing our Meaningful Mission, not from a place of trying to prove something to the rest of the world but by being of service to others while striving to be our best in our pursuits in life.

Our relationship
with money is
an emotionally
intense, intimate
relationship.

– Lewis Howes

TAKE YOURSELF TO MONEY THERAPY

Creating a healthy relationship with money is like a dance. You have to learn how to connect with your heart but not get carried away by emotion. You can't allow money to walk all over you, blind you, or take away your healthy boundaries in exchange for access to it.

You have to be able to ask tough questions and stay aligned with your personal values. You have to know when to go in depth and do your due diligence before you invest in something that has the potential to give you a great return.

That is why I suggest you engage in money therapy with yourself. It is important for you to understand that the persona you assign to money comes from you. It is not a unique person in and of itself; it reflects what you project onto it. **Change the way you see and feel about money and you change the way money interacts with you.**

Consequently, you need to make space to reflect on how you see and feel about money. There may be things you are ashamed of, embarrassed by, or afraid to talk about. The first step is simply to bring them into the light. Doing so will help you find patterns of behavior based on triggers and help you bring awareness and clarity to why you do what you do with your money.

Let's start your healing journey:

1. **Identify your money triggers.** A friend of mine remembers when his parents told him they couldn't afford to buy fabric softener sheets, and so he presumed that people who could must be rich. Now, even as an adult, the scent of dryer sheets reminds him of his limiting perspective that money just wasn't available for people like him. It's a story of lack, not abundance.

   Your trigger may be less tactile in nature and more emotional. For example, if you do not have enough money to pay an upcoming bill, emotions may flare up that stem from arguments your parents had about paying bills when you were a child. As a result, you splurge on a shopping spree to feel better or make panicked moves with investments to try to get that bill paid.

Think about what emotional triggers you have around money. What stories are attached to them?

2. **Write it down.** Journaling is a great way to get your thoughts and feelings out in a way you can observe them better. Try to keep a journal for a week or two and note every time you have an emotional reaction to something involving money.

As you read what you wrote down, you might be surprised by the thoughts and reasons that pop up to explain why you do the things you do with money. Don't judge what you write; just let it out and see what surfaces.

3. **Talk to a safe person.** Trust me; keeping things bottled up doesn't help you in the long run. Talking out loud about what you're going through helps you process the information. Getting it out into the open (whether it's with a therapist or coach, spiritual advisor, or even speaking to a trusted friend) can emotionally set you free. This release gives you the peace you deserve.

However, I do suggest you be intentional about choosing the person and make sure they have a positive relationship with money. Otherwise, you may be exposing yourself to negative input from their own poor relationship with it.

4. **Forgive yourself and others.** There is a place for forgiveness in any kind of therapy. Whatever mistakes you have made with money in the past—and we've all made them—you must learn from them and then let them go. A big part of forgiving yourself in money therapy involves letting go of the feelings of guilt and shame that you have held on to for too long.

You can forgive yourself for those times when you used money in a way that did not align with your higher self. For those times when you suppressed your natural Money Style and went against what felt right to you. For those times when you did not take care of your money and then were disappointed when your money did not take care of you. Back then, you didn't have the emotional tools to feel safe, so you did things from anxiety, stress, and survival mode. Now, as you take the journey to heal yourself, you are healing your relationship with money as well. Let go in order to level up.

If I hadn't learned to forgive myself and find ways to integrate the healing lessons I've learned, I would have continued to have an emotional reaction because that wound is still there. Until we heal those wounds and start integrating the healing journey, we'll continue to feel like we're in emotional fight-or-flight mode around money.

5. **Practice overcoming your triggers.** Once you release the negative emotions associated with your Money Story, you open up to more positive actions flowing from you. After you identify the things that trigger certain emotions toward money, you'll be able to notice when you start to react in the old way and you'll make a different choice. Then it's simply a matter of practicing your new responses to those triggers.

   For example, perhaps in the past when your significant other said something that you interpreted as implying you were not making wise money decisions, it flashed you back to a parent or someone else who mattered berating you for your money failures. Rather than reacting to your partner from that place of hurt and regret, you can acknowledge the trigger, see the situation through your healed relationship with money, remove emotion from the conversation, and respond in a healthy way by asking questions to learn more.

6. **Create healthy boundaries.** You likely need to have some courageous conversations with people you care about to put healthy boundaries in place. For example, there have been times when I've given money to people for a certain purpose only to discover it was used in a different way than we agreed. As tough as it was, I had to have that conversation to let them know that their behavior was not okay with me. We were no longer in emotional alignment. We had to start over and create a new agreement to try to rebuild the trust.

    In these types of conversations, you have to be clear about what you want, the energy you want to feel, and the type of peace you want to have as a result. In every relationship there are exchanges of value, including exchanges that are not explicitly about money. Remember, boundaries aren't designed to restrict you; instead, the right ones are there to make you feel safe and set you free.

7. **Motivate yourself to grow.** I like games, so I always look for little ways to gamify a situation when I need to be motivated to overcome something. Maybe when you see yourself making a wise move with money from a healed place, you treat yourself to a little something that is meaningful to you.

    It doesn't have to be something that costs money, or even some *thing*. It could be just telling yourself out loud that you did a great job. It could be giving yourself the gift of time in a soothing bath. It could even be relational in nature, such as grabbing coffee with someone or visiting a spa together. The key is to set up little ways to reward yourself and motivate yourself to engage with money differently.

You can't just heal your relationship with money and leave the rest of yourself a mess. When I released pain from my old wounds and became free energetically, I could finally focus on the things that mattered. When something that used to trigger me showed up in my life again, I was able to notice it and respond to it differently. I could say no to things, create boundaries, and break through barriers. I eliminated meetings I didn't want to take because I didn't feel like I had to be a people pleaser anymore.

Everything started to fade away that was tied to my thoughts of *I don't feel like I'm enough, so let me do things for others and avoid disturbing or upsetting people.* I chose to focus on my mission, health, and relationships so I could show up with clarity and intentionality.

In their wildly popular book, *Attached*, Amir Levine and Rachel S. F. Heller explore three primary types of relationship styles. Two are negative: avoidant and anxious. One is positive: secure.

If we layer these relationship styles on top of our Money Styles and Story, we can better understand our relationship with money. Someone with an avoidant approach tends to devalue money and treat it as something to steer clear of. Even though that person may actually really want it, they unconsciously do all they can to make sure it doesn't come their way. Someone with an anxious approach treats money the exact opposite way: they fret about it, worry over it, cling to every penny, and generally live a frustrated life in relationship with it. They seek something money can never truly give: affirmation of their own value.

Someone who has a healthy relationship with money has a secure relationship with themselves first. They are secure in the sense that they are neither avoiding money nor anxious about it. They project confidence into the universe around money, and in return, money tends to come to them more easily.

It was only when I did the work to heal myself and become more secure that I could then heal my relationship with money. And that's when I truly began to understand the role money played in fulfilling my Meaningful Mission.

By learning to understand and heal your traumas and triggers, you can give yourself permission to move forward in a more powerful way, walking in integrity and alignment with your agreements and making money for the purpose of fulfilling your Meaningful Mission.

YOUR GAME PLAN

Exercise 1: Act Your Way to Belief

If you want to heal your relationship with money, you've got to change your beliefs. But this is often easier said than done. A counterintuitive way to do this is to change your actions first and then watch as new beliefs form around those actions.

To put this into practice, create a chart that explores your healing and harmful actions, and your positive and negative thoughts. Write any negative thoughts you may have around money in the bottom left quadrant. These are the thoughts you want to eliminate. In the bottom right corner, identify the harmful actions these thoughts have caused.

In the top left corner, write any healing actions you can take around money. In the top right corner, write the corresponding positive thought that action creates. As you begin to recognize the relationship between your thoughts and actions, you can look for ways to take more healing actions than harmful actions and to think more positive thoughts than negative thoughts. This is a powerful way for you to begin to heal.

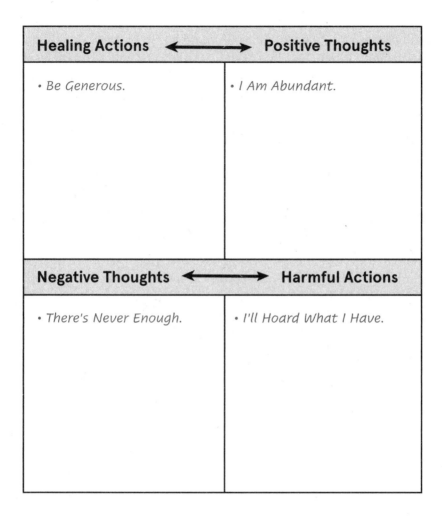

Healing Actions ←——→ Positive Thoughts	
• Be Generous.	• I Am Abundant.

Negative Thoughts ←——→ Harmful Actions	
• There's Never Enough.	• I'll Hoard What I Have.

Exercise 2: Let Go and Level Up

Healing any relationship requires knowing what to let go of and then having the courage to do it. On the other side of this are the lightness and freedom you've been missing. In order to level up, you've got to learn to let go.

This exercise is aspirational. It requires some honest reflection and self-awareness. Find a quiet spot to sit. Clear away distractions. Once you are dialed in, think about the unhelpful thoughts, beliefs, and feelings you carry about money. Identify these thoughts, beliefs, and feelings. Name them. This is the baggage that weighs you down. Then determine to let them go. As you do, visualize a lighter you. Where will this newfound lightness enable you to level up? Get aspirational. Dream big dreams. Make your vision concrete.

As a final step, write it down. How are you feeling now? Make it present tense so it feels like it's something you can start thinking/believing/feeling tomorrow. Take this lightness with you as you heal your money relationship. This is critical as you move into the next chapter and see how money connects to your Meaningful Mission.

Exercise 3: Find a Money Mentor

Who do you know who has a healthy relationship with money? It helps to learn from people who are several steps ahead of you in your journey. Think about the people you know who have a good relationship with money and whose Money Story and Style you admire.

Then reach out. Book a lunch or coffee with them. Interview them. Get a new perspective. Borrow their belief. When you are finished, journal about what you learned from them, and let them know how it impacted your thinking. If it makes sense (and if they are willing and able), set up a recurring time to meet and discuss your evolving relationship with money. As you make more money, it will be important to have money mentors who can guide you on the different opportunities and challenges money may bring you.

CHAPTER FIVE

MONEY AND YOUR MEANINGFUL MISSION

What scares you about making more money? A lot of people I've talked to are afraid of who they'll become if they grow wealthy. When was the last time you watched a show where the richest person was also the most generous person? Probably not lately. Instead, people with money are often portrayed as being uncaring, callous, and often downright evil.

But remember, money doesn't decide who you are; it simply reveals more of who you already are. This is why wisdom literature across the ages has emphasized that money itself is not bad, but loving it to the exclusion of other good things is when things go wrong. Said another way, when our relationship with money is off, it disrupts our pursuit of a richer life.

Money is merely a tool, a way to store value. It is also a catalyst, an amplifying or multiplying force—especially with regard to your ability to do great good in the world. Ironically, any relationship problems you have with money tend to come to the surface, even when you try to do something meaningful with it.

For example, suppose you have a passion for helping people get physically fit so they will live longer, healthier lives. If you have an avoidant approach in your relationship with money, you might struggle to charge enough for your services. As a result, you can't make ends meet and must get a nine-to-five job you don't like. On the other hand, if you tend to have a more anxious approach, you might fall into unhealthy lifestyle patterns as you worry and fret over being able to pay the bills. As a result, your business suffers alongside you, and you have to go back to an occupation that doesn't align with your mission. Different relationship reasons but the same result. But if you are secure in your relationship with money, you'll find it easier to connect money with what matters most to you—your Meaningful Mission.

In my book *The Greatness Mindset*, I unpack this concept of finding your Meaningful Mission in greater depth. It lays a strong foundation for who you need to become to have a vibrant relationship with money—and with everyone else, for that matter. For a mission to be *meaningful*, it must first be personal to you. It must resonate with you individually. It can't be a mission someone else wants you to tackle. It can't be imposed on you against your will. It must be an intentional embrace of a direction that is significant to you.

And that is key because it means no one else can choose your Meaningful Mission for you. Bob Goff, best-selling author of *Love Does*, puts it this way: "I used to be afraid of failing at the things that really mattered to me, but now I'm more afraid of succeeding at things that don't matter."[1] Blockbuster actor Jim Carrey says, "You can fail at what you don't want, so you might as well take a chance on doing what you love."[2] When what you do truly matters to you, you tend to live life with no regrets.

Your Meaningful Mission taps into something more significant in life. It calls upon the deeper parts of your soul and moves you to attempt something greater than yourself. Like a heroic quest, this mission has a singular focus or purpose, as well as a call that compels you to push through resistance to complete it. It often remakes the people who are part of it into something better. And it always implies that the destination is grander or greater than any you have previously achieved. After all, if it's something you have done before and could easily do again, it's not much of a mission.

At the time of this writing, my Meaningful Mission remains unchanged from when I wrote it in *The Greatness Mindset*:

> To serve 100 million lives weekly by helping them improve the quality of their lives and overcome the things that hold them back.

What, you may be asking, *does my Meaningful Mission have to do with money?* A lot. Here's why: money multiplies your ability to fulfill your mission. Put simply, if I had no money, I would struggle greatly to reach anyone, let alone 100 million people. It takes money to create an incredible show, to hire a team, and to share compelling media with people all over the world. To scale my message of hope, growth, and inspiration, I need money for resources to make it happen. The more money I make and the clearer I get on my mission, the more people I can help.

And the same is true for you: money can make your Meaningful Mission come alive.

THE PRIORITY PENDULUM

There are two ways you can go about this. You can start with making money and then finding your mission. Or you can start by finding your mission and then monetizing it.

I've seen both approaches work. For example, billionaire Mark Cuban has stated publicly that it is foolish to follow your passion in an attempt to become wealthy. He suggests you follow the money first and then use that money to do good in the world in alignment with your mission.

I know it worked for me in those early years when I just needed to make more money as I figured out my mission. The problem was that I had not healed my relationship with money, or with myself, for that matter. Looking back now, I can see that if I had had more clarity on my mission and devoted more time and energy into healing my relationships on all fronts, I could have accelerated that growth curve and made more money more easily.

Money can make your Meaningful Mission come alive.

— Lewis Howes

One concern I have with this money-first focus is that it may prevent us from living our most authentic lives. When we are doing what doesn't fulfill us, we tend to get empty quickly. That doesn't mean it has to happen, but there can be a danger of living an inauthentic life.

Another possible danger of focusing solely on making money is that if you have not healed your relationship with it, you can easily get off course. If the choices that drive your mission are fueled solely by wanting more money, it will be tough to sustain your drive to pursue it. Or you may make compromises with your personal values in order to make more money, and you may never feel you are making enough. On top of that, your Money Story may harmfully amplify or suppress your natural Money Style, leading you to poor decisions and an even worse quality of life. Add to that any avoidant or anxious relationship tendencies you have, and you could have some serious challenges ahead.

On the other side of what I call the Priority Pendulum is the approach that says to focus solely on your passion and the money will inevitably follow. I've got to admit this approach really resonates with me. I am so motivated today by what I'm passionate about, and this is where my heart naturally goes. However, I don't think it always works all that well in the real world. We all know starving artists who are doing what they love but no one knows about them. How much better would the world be if they had money to promote their work? Or what about an aspiring entrepreneur who has an idea that could really make the world a better place but has no funding to make it happen? Or a crusader trying to cure an injustice in the world without any donors to support the cause?

Passion alone is not enough. Neither is chasing money. The missing link is the skill you don't yet have but absolutely need if you're ever going to monetize your Meaningful Mission. Maybe a starving artist is afraid to promote himself because then he would be "selling out." But really he just needs to learn skills in marketing, sales, networking, and collaboration in order to get his message out to others. Likewise, a skilled carpenter who has a passion for building things in her garage needs to learn sales and marketing if her woodwork is going to produce money.

Don't let the *how* stop you from focusing on and pursuing your *why*.

— Lewis Howes

Don't get me wrong. I think passion is a smart place to start.

If I had to do it over again, I would start with my Meaningful Mission first and then seek to make money in a way that aligns with it—and this is key—*as best I could in that season of life.* I know that for me, once I began to get crystal clear on my Meaningful Mission, that mission led the way, and money has followed. But I have had to develop the skills I needed along the way and the disciplines to deploy the Money Habits to monetize the mission effectively.

Ask yourself: *If money were no longer an issue, what would I do? What would light me up every day?* Don't let the *how* stop you from focusing on and pursuing your *why.* Once you have clarity on your *why,* then you can seek that middle zone on the Priority Pendulum.

The Priority Pendulum

The Money Focus

The Passion Focus

The Meaningful Mission Zone

The Money Focus

- Expects to get to passions later
- Focuses on making money first

The Passion Focus

- Follows what you love to do
- Trusts that money will follow

The Meaningful Mission Zone

- Driven by mission
- Adapts to your season of life
- Seeks alignment between money and mission
- Learns skills needed to succeed
- Overcomes fears of monetizing the mission

Most people will find the most success in that middle place where their passion and money and reality come together. There will likely be seasons of life when you must do something you don't fully love just to make money until you can transition to something you do love that aligns with your mission. And that's okay. Instead of beating yourself up in that season, give yourself the freedom to make money in those ways. But don't lose sight of your mission. The goal is to always be moving toward achieving greater alignment between money and your Meaningful Mission.

ALIGNING WITH YOUR WHY

Why do you want to make money? Is it so you can eventually pursue your passions? Is it to fund your passion right now? Is your motivation in alignment with your Meaningful Mission? Or is it more about ego and caring about what other people think of you?

On the other hand, maybe you don't want to make more money at all. If you consciously or unconsciously believe you are not enough—not good enough, not smart enough, not talented enough, not worthy enough—then I guarantee you will consistently make decisions that don't align with the highest version of yourself. You might accomplish great things and generate amazing results, but if you don't learn the process of overcoming self-doubt through healing, you'll always feel stress or pain in your heart. You'll continue to feel like something's off. Your life may be good, but it won't be great. You'll be stuck, and the road out is a long journey. I know. I've taken it.

I once thought my purpose in life was to play professional football and get paid to do what I loved. I only made $250 a week playing in the Arena Football League. The team paid for my apartment, but I had to live off food stamps to survive. Even though I was financially poor, I felt rich because I was living my dream. I carpooled to practices and games with teammates who had cars. It felt great to earn a paycheck for something that had been a goal of mine for so long. I felt like I was living my life *on mission,* and the goal was to continue to get better so I could make more.

When the pro football chapter of my life ended, I became a connector of ideas, people, and solutions through in-person events and LinkedIn, learning about the platform by trial and error. I invested time discovering, testing, and trying things to build an audience. Then I realized I could make money by sharing what I learned. I wasn't sure if it was my Meaningful Mission, but I leaned in to the clarity and skill set I had to find a new way to pay the bills. I decided to see how far I could take it. I started with one-on-one consulting. That turned into in-person events, a book, and even an online training course.

Helping people with LinkedIn was a season that brought in the money to get me off my sister's couch. But although I had created a life of service to other people and enjoyed what I was doing, it wasn't my ultimate dream. A greater mission waited for me out there. When I had made enough money through my marketing work, I started *The School of Greatness* show and soon found myself right in that sweet spot of the Meaningful Mission zone.

You may be in a season where you need money to get back on your feet. You don't have to feel bad or embarrassed about that. If you heal your relationship with money, live out of a place of mission, and act on the Money Habits that I'll share with you, you may be better equipped to monetize your Meaningful Mission.

MONETIZE YOUR MISSION

It is okay to make money in pursuit of your mission. I know that to some people, that statement might sound wrong. Maybe you're thinking, *I don't care about money, Lewis. I just want to help people.* But more money gives you more resources to serve more people.

Jay Shetty, *New York Times* best-selling author of *Think Like a Monk,* and I love to meet up regularly and discuss deep questions. We had decided to record an episode of my show in which we asked this awkward question—"Can you make money and be spiritual at the same time?" Jay and I grew up in different parts of the world, but it didn't take long to realize we shared similar beliefs about the answer. I too knew a lot of people who grew up believing you can either be like Mother Teresa or some kind of money-hungry criminal at the root of all evil.

Where Jay grew up, people believed that if someone was wealthy, they must have "done something dodgy or bad to get there." After living as a monk for many years in India in his twenties, Jay started creating videos teaching people what he had learned about life as a monk. He was on a mission to share the wisdom he had gained from his experiences and observations to help people think differently about life.

At that point, he wasn't sure making money was something he could do. He questioned whether he could be spiritual and make money at the same time. Although his videos had hundreds of millions of views, Jay struggled financially. When he was four months away from losing his apartment, he realized the situation was negatively affecting the long-term impact he could sustainably have on the world. He challenged his beliefs so he could make more money *and* serve at a greater level while also investing in the necessities for himself—a comfortable sleeping space, better nutrition, and giving himself a chance to hire a larger team so he could scale his message and get it out to more people.

It is okay to make money in pursuit of your mission.

— Lewis Howes

Jay asked some powerful questions inspired by his own wrestling with the balance between money and spirituality:

> If we're saying that spiritual people can't be rich, that means that spiritual people have to be poor. That means all the people that are rich are not spiritual. Is that the world we want to live in?
>
> Do we want to live in a world where the wealthiest people or the people who have the most resources are people who don't have spiritual intentions? I would rather grow up in a world where the most influential people had a deep spiritual intention.[3]

For me, spirituality is about harmony and having inner peace. And if you're financially struggling, feeling stuck, or trapped in debt, there is a good chance you are not experiencing inner peace. Just the opposite. In fact, your lack of money may be holding you back from making spiritual progress.

It's true that some people use money in a selfish way. But what if we could challenge the prevailing narrative and use money to make the world a better place? Take Oprah Winfrey, for example. Her conversations on her show have shifted the thinking of millions of people. And you probably know wealthy people in your own community who have created scholarships, funded world-changing organizations, or made your city a better place to live. Those people didn't just have big hearts; they had big bank accounts to go with them.

I understand why you may think that money shouldn't be your only focus, and I agree. But money can multiply your ability to fulfill your Meaningful Mission. You can do what you love and potentially make money at the same time. When you understand your Meaningful Mission, there is nothing wrong with aiming to make money to fund it. It is possible to strive for your greatest impact in a high-paying career or by creating a profitable business that aligns with your Meaningful Mission.

THINK A LITTLE DIFFERENTLY

One example of someone who has done this is Timothy Sykes. At 21 years old, he became a self-made millionaire by using his bar mitzvah money to begin a stock-trading career. In a philanthropy course at Tulane University, he became a wish granter for the Make-A-Wish Foundation, where he continues to donate. He also used money he made as a penny-stock trader during his senior year to donate a scholarship to the college.

But he wanted to do more, so he worked with a team to create the Timothy Sykes Foundation. His Meaningful Mission grew beyond giving to collaborating with other donors to create a greater impact than he could ever have on his own.

On my show he was excited to announce that he would donate $1 million to a charity I support, Pencils of Promise. That's a lot of money for anyone, but Tim told me he understands that it's about so much more than the money: "I know a lot of people want to discuss the headline number, donating a million dollars—fantastic stuff. But it's about what your money can do. And if you don't have money, what can you do to help an organization?"

Tim has bought every expensive thing he could buy with money. He has traveled first class and on private jets to more than 100 different countries all over the world. He has dined at the most exclusive restaurants and bought his fill of clothes, watches, and cars. But at the end of the day, he says that stuff isn't what life is about. For Tim, all those toys are fun, but they aren't fulfilling:

> If you're unhappy out there, you need to think a little differently. Aside from just the money you can make, what can you do with your life? What is your life about?[4]

I couldn't agree more. You can have goals and dreams, but those goals and dreams can sometimes be based on what's going to make you look and feel good. Your intention may be more ego-based. Maybe you want to make your parents proud, impress others, or stand out among your friends. It's easy to compare what you're doing with what your friends do and feel like you must meet or exceed their success.

But when you create a Meaningful Mission that empowers others, it becomes renewable energy for yourself. When life gets tough, you feel like you can wake up every morning and do challenging things because there's something bigger at play than just serving yourself.

Now if you're ready to make more money to help you fulfill your Meaningful Mission, you'll soon discover the 7 Money Habits I have developed from countless conversations with experts, extensive research, and my own life and business experiences. For clarity, let me repeat my intention that these habits, while powerful, are for guidance in growth and not financial advice.

Let's go make more money—and help a lot more people along the way!

YOUR GAME PLAN

Exercise 1: The Multiplier Effect

Money doesn't decide who you are; it reveals who you are. And who you already are is enough to do amazing things in the world. Let's create a chart to identify some of your best qualities and ways you *currently* serve humanity. It's okay to brag!

In one column, write a list of positive qualities about you—for example, things you do to serve others, gifts and skills you use to make the world a better place, ways you like to be generous, or causes you are passionate about.

In a corresponding column, write how having more money will help you multiply the effect of your greatness. Write it in the present tense, for example: "Because I am wealthy and abundant, I am able to give regular monthly donations to the pet shelter."

This exercise helps you connect your Meaningful Mission with your money and tells the universe that you are ready!

Ways I'm Awesome *Now*	How Money Will Help Me Serve More
I feel so much joy when I give my time to serve at the local pet shelter.	Because I am wealthy and abundant, I am able to give regular monthly donations to the pet shelter in addition to my time volunteering. With this gift, they can add more staff and purchase a new piece of equipment.

Exercise 2: How Could My Money Make the World a Better Place?

It's time to dream about how money plus your Meaningful Mission can make the world a better place. Everyone is uniquely positioned to make a difference—that includes you. Use the prompts below to sketch a back-of-a-napkin "business plan" for how you would use money to make the world a better place. Pretend you're having a friendly dinner with Timothy Sykes and he's asking you how you would use $1 million to serve others. What would you say?

The Person. *Who would you help? Describe that person or group in detail.*

The Problem. *What problem are they facing?*

The Pain. *What pain are they experiencing as a result of that problem? How does it affect their life?*

The Prescription. *What would you do to help them? How would you make that pain go away?*

The Pathway. *What solution would you provide for them? How would they use your solution to solve their problem?*

The Power. *How would your solution empower them to become different and/or better?*

The Payoff. *What will their life look like as a result of your solution? How will they be able to help others? How will this make the world a better place?*

STEP 3

Prepare for More Money

Now it's time to get tactical by harnessing the power of the 7 Money Habits. Each habit is powerful on its own, but, as you can see in the illustration on page 98, dramatic change happens when they build on one another. That's why Step 3 is all about leveraging these powerful habits to help you prepare to receive more money. As always, don't try to live my unique story or think that if you do what I did, you'll automatically have a lot of money in the bank. I'm still a work in progress, just like you. But these powerful habits can help you become a better version of yourself and heal your relationship with money so you can be best positioned to enjoy a richer life.

Find more free resources to accelerate your growth and make money easy at MakeMoneyEasyBook.com.

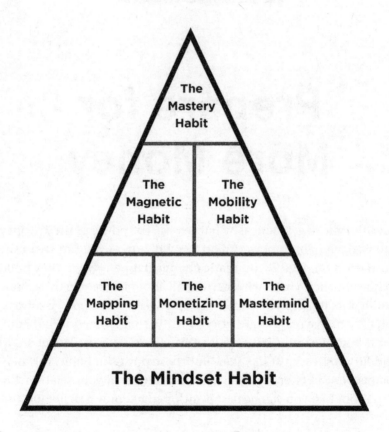

CHAPTER SIX

HABIT 1: THE MINDSET HABIT

Live Generously

Gratitude is the gateway to abundance.

When I went to my first mastermind event many years ago, I was just getting some traction doing LinkedIn training. It was a small weekend event with no more than 20 people. But these weren't just any random people. They were all successful entrepreneurs or business owners with multimillion-dollar companies—some making eight or nine figures in annual revenue. While I knew I was still young and new in business, trying to figure things out, I knew the only way to grow was to be around people much wiser and more experienced than I was.

Despite feeling intimidated and fearful, I did the only thing I knew to do at the time. I jumped in and started helping other members with their LinkedIn strategy. "Hey, let me fix this for you. Happy to do that for you." I didn't ask for any money. I didn't have any ulterior motive. I was sincerely just trying to be helpful.

By the end of that weekend, I had built quality relationships with five of the attendees. After the event I followed up with them, asking how else I could be of service with their LinkedIn and social media strategy. They were so inspired by what they were learning and how it would directly help them build their businesses that they wanted to do more with me. They each had audiences and wanted me to teach their audiences what I had taught them.

So they followed up with offers: "Hey, what you did was so powerful. I'd love to do a webinar with you. Can you teach this to my audience?" Within the next three months, I had done five webinars and brought in half a million dollars of business. Up to that point, the most I had generated in a year was a quarter of a million. This opened my eyes to an entirely new world, and my business—and my life—would never be the same.

What I learned from that experience was that if I wanted to make more money, I needed to lean in to being generous and think about serving others first. If you want your bank account balance to go up and live a richer life, you must be willing to give up your resources, knowledge, talent, time, and energy. That is true whether you're advancing a career, starting a business of your own, or trying to move forward with anything in this world. In my experience, success starts to accelerate when you begin to give.

The flip side of being generous is being grateful. Gratitude sparks the drive to create, attract, and manifest more. A generous heart is a grateful heart. The two are inseparable—but if you give from a place of guilt or feeling like you have to, then you aren't being grateful. If gratitude is the doorway to a richer life, generosity is how you walk through it to make it real in the world. Gratitude brings an abundance of joy, positive emotions, good energy, and deep fulfillment. And when you have more fulfillment, you feel more whole. As a result, you're able to attract money and all other potentially positive things from a healthier place.

You can always practice gratitude, even when you don't have money or anything else to give. That's why it should be a daily practice from the moment you wake up. When you're with someone, you can easily express it outwardly—and for free. You can also express gratitude within, just by thinking, *I'm grateful for . . .* It's not uncommon for me to walk outside my front door on a sunny day, put my arms up, and think, *I'm so grateful for all I've been given.*

Success starts
to accelerate
when you
begin to give.

— Lewis Howes

Generosity begins with a grateful heart and mindset that puts you in a place of positivity so you are poised to give and to receive. When you're in a state of thankfulness, you are more likely to be generous. If you're in a state of ingratitude, a place where you lack appreciation, you're less likely to want to give to others. When you are frustrated with or unloving toward yourself, you're less likely to collaborate, support, and help others.

Some people treat these principles like a magic formula and try to force it, thinking if they just put in a dollar of giving, they'll receive two dollars back the next day. But that's not how this works. This first Money Habit—the Mindset Habit—requires you believing that whatever good you put out into the world will come back to you as better in some way at some later time.

Establishing a generous and grateful Mindset Habit positions you to multiply and magnify the impact of each habit to follow as you embark on the path to living a richer, more abundant life.

THE POWER OF GRATITUDE

A grateful life is a richer life. The science is straightforward in support of the connection between gratitude and happiness.

Dr. Laurie Santos, former head of Silliman College at Yale and host of *The Happiness Lab* podcast, developed an interest in the science of happiness from wanting to help stressed-out college students. Laurie began teaching a class on happiness called The Science of Well-Being with a focus on the science of happiness, common misconceptions we have about happiness, and practical ways to implement happiness. The class had to be scheduled in a concert hall to accommodate its whopping enrollment of 1,200 students!

When I interviewed Laurie on *The School of Greatness*, she shared a study with me of people who were given $20 and told they either had to spend it or give it away to someone else by the end of the day. It turns out that at the end of the day, those who spent the money on someone else felt better than those who spent it on themselves.[1]

A grateful life is a richer life.

— Lewis Howes

Generous people are grateful people. Grateful people are happier people. Happier people attract more opportunities.

To help identify how to act with generosity, it can be incredibly clarifying to ask this question: *What would a generous person do?* For example, when I am in a church service, I might typically give some money. But when I ask myself this question, I find myself answering that a generous person would give more. Not out of a sense of duty or obligation but as an expression of who I am. I choose to be a generous person, and so I give.

That isn't always easy to do. When business is down and the economy is filled with uncertainty, many of us know what might be coming next. However, when I live from a place of faith and not fear, I can choose to respond generously.

It's not about how much you give but that you are the kind of person who *does* give. For some people, that might be a dollar or two. For others, it might be thousands or even millions. The person who stretches to give $2 is no less worthy than the one who stretches to give 2 million. If each approaches money with a generous heart and open hands, they position themselves to interact with the universe as someone who can be trusted with money.

Be aware of where your energy is flowing. If it feels authentic to you, and you feel good about giving, you will want to do it. If you feel taken advantage of or if it feels out of alignment with who you are, you won't want to do it. No matter what pressure you may be facing, either internally or externally, make sure you're good with yourself first and in alignment with your relationship with money.

Most situations in life do not involve money, at least not directly. That's why it can be helpful to ask another clarifying question: *What would a grateful person do?* If you live in awareness of how much you've been given and in appreciation for how much has come to you—and trust that more is going to come—then giving some money, time, energy, or attention right now won't limit you from creating more.

When you have faith in your values, live consistently with your identity, and trust in your abilities, you should be able to create more opportunities for money by using your resources in alignment with who you are and who you are becoming.

PLANT GENEROSITY SEEDS

When I was a young kid, my father would take my two sisters and me on an hour's drive to Camp Willson, a YMCA camp in Bellefontaine, Ohio. During these family camp weekends, I loved swimming and fishing in the pond, participating in outdoor activities, and just being part of the beautiful natural setting. But on one hot summer day, we didn't go to camp to play or swim in the lake. We went to plant trees.

As we pulled into the campgrounds early in the morning, there was an empty field that was hilly and full of dirt, and a big pickup truck loaded with thousands of foot-tall seedling trees and several small hand shovels. My dad rallied us around the truck and told us that it's our responsibility as humans to be in service to the communities we live in and pay it forward whenever we can.

He told us this was an opportunity to give back to the place that brought our family so much joy and that one day, long after we were gone, these trees would bring beauty, inspiration, and shade to animals and people for decades and potentially centuries to come, and they would enrich the campgrounds.

As a nine-year-old, I wasn't inspired by this speech. Standing in Ohio's 100-degree summer weather, all I could think about was how stupid it was to be on my hands and knees digging up dirt to put these trees in the ground when I could be jumping in the cool lake.

We spent the entire day there, and by the end of it, we had planted over 1,000 trees in rows along this field. At first, I mostly complained, but my dad wisely turned it into a game and a competition, which eventually gave me something else to focus on.

For the next 10 years, we went back and saw these little trees sprout up slowly, but the little forest still didn't look like much. After my father's car accident and traumatic brain injury, I stopped going back to the campground. Only after he passed away just a few years ago did I again visit Camp Willson. It was 30 years since we had planted those trees.

As I pulled into the campground driveway, I was amazed to see an entire forest of trees, each standing 30 to 50 feet high, hugging the campgrounds. I couldn't help but think about that day as a young boy with my dad teaching me a valuable lesson about life, about gratitude, and about being of service.

An ancient proverb says something to this effect: "The true meaning of life is to plant trees under whose shade you do not expect to sit." It works in both directions. I may plant seeds by being generous to others today. I may not even directly benefit from planting those seeds, but someone will. Likewise, I'll experience the happiness that comes from sitting in the shade of a tree someone else planted but never directly enjoyed. Sometimes you get to plant the seeds; sometimes you get to enjoy the shade of the trees that grew from those seeds.

Perhaps that is why so many sources of great wisdom affirm that it is better to give than to receive. We may experience external benefits, but by giving, we are always assured of experiencing a richer life because of the internal growth and peace that take place within us.

I have faith that whatever I give away will come back to me in some fashion. It may come back as an abundance of money—ten, a hundred, or even a thousand times over. Or it may come back to me in the form of deepened relationships, memories, peace, joy, or a variety of other ways to create a richer life for me and those I love.

The reality is that none of us can take our money with us when we die. The wealthiest person in the world will leave it all behind. Instead of holding on to it, what if that person used their money generously to plant seeds? They may not be able to control what grows from those seeds, but they can control when, where, and how they are planted, which is far more than they can do after their time on earth is done.

Tony Robbins, who I have interviewed many times on my show, tells his own story that illustrates this secret. He was 17 years old, sleeping in the back of his car and working 18-hour days to make ends meet. Someone owed him thousands of dollars, but he wasn't able to collect. With just $26 to his name, he decided to splurge on one final all-you-can-eat meal at a buffet nearby.

Tony was pocketing his $17 in change when he saw a sharply dressed young boy come in with a woman who seemed to be his mother. He was impressed as he watched the boy act like a gentleman. On his way out, he stopped to let the boy know what a delight it was to see him treating his mother to dinner. "Oh, I'm not treating her to dinner," the boy replied, "I don't have a job, so I don't actually have any money."

"You do now," Tony said as he placed his last $17 on the boy's table. As Tony describes it, he "flew" out of that restaurant, powered by the freedom he felt after giving away his last cent.

When he got home, what did he find in the mail? A letter from the person who owed him money, apologizing for not paying him. And a check for all the money he was owed.

Tony gave when he had nothing because he was learning to move beyond a scarcity mindset driven by fear and anger to embrace an abundance mindset driven by love and generosity. As he became the best version of himself, more money flowed his way and he was able to keep being generous.

The same is true for you. If you show yourself to be a good steward of money when you have little, money will naturally flow to you more. It knows it can trust you. And as you give more and more, and respond with more gratitude for all you have, that trust builds. You won't magically transform into a generous person someday. Start right now and show yourself to be a trusted partner for money.

The same is true of any resources you have, not just money. When I was just starting out helping people use LinkedIn, I gave away a lot of my time and expertise. I did countless free consultations, workshops, and meetings to help people who needed it.

Serving other people helped shape me into a healthier person as I simply helped other human beings. Plus, many of the generosity seeds I planted back then paid dividends later, especially in the early days of *The School of Greatness* when many of those people came on the show. I didn't do it for money, but money flowed to me because of my generosity.

I believe this is the way the universe works. If you want to make money easy, get good at giving it away. If you have not built a container of generosity and gratitude, then whatever you do manage to make will leak out and leave you empty and unfulfilled. Practice being generous with all you have—money, time, and skills—to be a collaborator with a willing heart and helping hands.

COMPOUNDING GENEROSITY

Let me be clear about one thing: this Mindset Habit is not a get-rich-quick plan. When you plant seeds, it can take time to see any fruit. That is why so many people skip it. They think they're taking a shortcut, but they are actually taking a detour that will lead them right back to the frustrated place where they started. Even if they do get more money, they end up unfulfilled, without the richer life they hoped money would give them.

If you want
to make
money easy,
get good at
giving it away.

— Lewis Howes

Ed Mylett, entrepreneur, podcaster, and best-selling author of *The Power of One More*, described a birthday party for a five-year-old. Every kid smacked the piñata with about the same force until one little girl finally broke it and made the candy go flying for everyone to enjoy and celebrate. His point? It took a sizable amount of compound pounding before the piñata broke.

"Most people don't wait around for the candy," Ed told me. "It takes time, but you're making invisible progress. If you ever start to get down or don't know what to do, give yourself credit for the compound pounding you're doing."[2]

"Can you survive the temporary?" Ed asked me, paraphrasing Napoleon Hill, author of *Think and Grow Rich*. "Here's what happens to most of us: we think everything's permanent. Because we think it's permanent, we make permanent decisions based on temporary conditions. Instead, say to yourself, *On the other side of this temporary pain is the other self.*"[3] That is the self you are becoming. You are enough, and you are becoming more. But you can never become more unless you are willing to give in a way that compounds to produce more.

My question for you is this: Are you willing to wait for the candy? To keep pounding every day, trusting that the person you are becoming and the seeds you are planting will pay off in a future richer life? Can you keep giving with a grateful heart, believing that a generous mindset will help you to make money easy?

Another example of the power of compound giving comes from Chris Anderson, head of TED and author of *Infectious Generosity*. As he explained to me, the TED Talk brand became so ubiquitous for one reason: they gave it away. When he had the opportunity to take over TED from its co-founder, Chris got excited about the program's potential to expand and share knowledge beyond its signature categories of technology, entertainment, and design (TED). So instead of purchasing the brand as a for-profit entity, he made TED part of his not-for-profit foundation and gave away the information to anyone who wanted it.

Although the conferences were exclusive, Chris decided the best way for the newly established nonprofit to run for the public good was for the events online to be shared *for free*. Anyone in the world could apply for a free license to put on a TED event. But they had to call it TEDx. Chris's foundation provided rules and tools and let the organizers do events where they wanted to and choose the speakers. This act of generosity and trust built the community.

The result was world-changing as now there are more than 70,000 people putting on TEDx events on their own time, without being paid, and at their own financial risk. They generate 25,000 videos a year and have introduced tremendous voices to us, such as Simon Sinek and Brené Brown, to name just a few.

TED gave away their brand and let people use it for free, again and again. As Chris told me, "We're going to give away our competitive secrets because we want the world to get better. We want others to learn from what we're using."[4]

BECOME A MONEY MAGNET

A big piece of the Mindset Habit is reprogramming yourself to think differently, not only when it comes to being generous and grateful but also changing the thought script you have around money. So many people unintentionally stop the flow of money to them.

"All the money everybody needs and wants is waiting there for them. And there's only one reason it's not in their lives. It's because they're stopping it from coming into their lives."[5] That's what Rhonda Byrne, author of the runaway bestseller *The Secret*, told me as we discussed money and the power of manifestation.Here are some ways you may be preventing money from coming to you:

1. **Thinking you don't have enough.** I remember the overwhelming stress about not having enough money to pay for things and thinking, *Am I ever going to make any money? Is it ever going to come to me?* That is when my mentor, Chris Hawker, told me, "Money comes to you when you're ready for it."

If the money had come to me then, I probably wouldn't have had it for long. I wouldn't have known how to invest it. I would've spent it poorly, or maybe I would've hoarded it because I was so afraid. But I wouldn't have known how to let it flow in and out of my life. And I probably would not have been quick to be generous with it.

At the core, the thought that I didn't have enough money really came down to my thinking that I was not enough. I had to do the work on myself before I could be ready to engage with money in a meaningful way.

2. **Thinking you don't deserve it.** You attract what you align yourself with. If you align yourself with scarcity, lack, and unworthiness, you'll continue to see more of that in your life. After all, if you truly do not deserve it, why would it make sense for money or anything good to come your way?

   It doesn't matter how much you say you want money. If you believe you don't deserve to have it, you'll find ways to stop it from coming to you. You might subconsciously sabotage opportunities for financial success or stay in your comfort zone and avoid any perceived risks that might lead to more money.

   When you see an opportunity to make more money, do you notice yourself procrastinating or doing things that keep you from taking advantage of it? Somewhere deep down, you may feel afraid of success. But when you align your beliefs about yourself with worthiness and abundance, you open yourself up to the flow of money and other blessings that you deserve.

3. **Believing negative money programming.** Negative Money Stories you hear as a child can subconsciously solidify into beliefs and behaviors that stop the flow of money in your adult life. For example, if you say you want to make more money but still think rich people are bad, you'll keep yourself from being a rich person.

What negative pieces of your Money Story no longer serve you? What might you be holding on to that needs to be replaced with a positive story? It takes work to change your story, but you owe it to yourself to make those changes.

My father used to mute the television when the commercials about medication or sickness came on as we watched sports as a family. He didn't want that program of illness, disease, and medication constantly running in my family's minds. Dad understood a profound truth: we start to believe the things we hear, and what we believe eventually becomes the truth for us.

As Rhonda Byrne says, "The Law of Attraction can only do what you believe."[6] Instead of letting negative things in, it's better to change the channel, adjust the conversation, switch your thoughts, or remove yourself from the situation. You need to stand guard over your mind to prevent thoughts and beliefs that won't serve you from taking up residence.

4. **Believing your current job is your only hope.** Maybe you saw your parents have one job for their entire lives. That was where all their money came from. Maybe everyone around you is trading hours for dollars in a way that's fulfilling for them, so you've grown used to thinking of making money in that way—and only in that way.

   The belief that there is only one way of doing things closes you off from other money-manifesting paths, such as starting a side gig, investing in various ways, creating passive income streams, or receiving an unexpected financial win. It also makes you afraid to fail, which means you likely won't take the risks needed to add more value and make more money.

   If you fear losing your job, you may never feel worthy enough to ask for a raise, take some time to relax, or learn a new skill that could help you get a promotion or open other doors. When you shift away from this belief, you can strengthen your financial well-being, take calculated risks, and open your mind to new opportunities for income streams.

When Rhonda Byrne was struggling financially, she repeated affirmations daily to retrain her mindset: *I have plenty of money. I attract whatever I need. I succeed at everything I touch.* She made it a point to express gratitude for the things she had and those that were on their way to her. She reversed anything that showed up as negative toward money to make it feel positive—including when it came time to pay the bills.

Every time she opened the mail and saw another stack of bills, her stomach would drop to her knees. But instead of owning that sense of dread, she learned that the Law of Attraction doesn't know or care if you're imagining something or if it's real. And that was when the games began.

When she opened a bill, she would grab a piece of paper and shout joyfully, "Whoa! I just got $1,200 in the mail!" Then she would open the next bill, exclaim how excited she was to receive the next amount due, and add the number to the list for the total of money that came to her that day. It got to a point where she didn't feel like she was receiving enough, so she added zeros to the amounts on her tally sheet to create an even larger total, exclaiming, *"Yes!* $150,000 is mine today!" Playing the game made her feel better, and then she would sit down and pay what she could using another game.

Instead of looking at her bill as an expense, she imagined that the money was a donation to the company. For example, "This company has been great by supplying me with electricity, so I'm making a donation. This money will help the people working at the company educate their children, buy food, and pay their mortgages." By reasoning that the pretend donation was on its way to doing good things for the company's employees, Rhonda shifted the way she felt about money. She reframed paying bills as an act of generosity.

When she got her bank statements, they were anything but pretty. Both her credit cards were maxed out, and she had no way of paying them off. So she took her marker to the statements, added four zeros to the balance due, and wrote "Thank You. Paid."[7]

Her playful solution reminds me of what Alan Watts said: "This is the real secret of life. To be completely engaged with what you are doing in the here and now. And instead of calling it work, realize it is play."[8]

Likewise, when Ken Honda was 19 years old, he came to the United States with just a little money in his bank account and set off on a one-year experiment. His plan was to explore the "kindness factor" and rely on the generosity of the people he met. For example, he once asked a man in a park if there was a restaurant nearby where he could eat for little to no money. Not only did the man take him to a place to eat, but he also paid for Ken's meal. Then he invited Ken to stay at his home after discovering he didn't have a place of his own.

At the end of the year, Ken had the same amount of money he had brought with him from Japan. He never went hungry and always had a place to sleep each night. That was back in 1987, and Ken still loves to pay forward the generosity he received then. He looks out for young American tourists when he sees them in other countries and pays for their meals.[9]

Ken told me what he sees as the key to serving the world around you:

> Instead of feeling overwhelmed by the bills, you can be creative and come up with ideas that you can contribute to the world. If you are more creative about serving the world and serving other people with your gifts, with who you are, you can create the flow of happy money. As a result, you can receive more money.[10]

Hear me when I say I'm not advocating for you to "act as if" and go into astronomical debt by doing fun things you can't yet afford or giving away all your money. But when you can find ways to flip the script and release playful energy toward money, it can help you become a money magnet.

PRACTICE YOUR GRATITUDE

Here are a few simple daily practices to develop your generosity muscle and to practice a more grateful mindset.

1. **Give money away.** When you go to your local coffee shop, be present with the people who are there. If you notice someone who feels magnetic, give them some money. It can be the barista making your drink or a patron who shares a smile with you. And it doesn't have to be a wild amount of money. It could be the penny you found in the cup holder of your car or the five-dollar bill in your pocket. By sharing your wealth and positive attitude with others, you invite the Law of Attraction to bring more back to you.

2. **Enjoy finding money.** Before you leave the house, decide on the amount of money that you'll discover while you're out and about. Again, it could be a penny, a dollar, or whatever you want. Then stay open to the possibility. When you find money, as Ken Honda suggests, thank it for coming and ask where it would like to go.

3. **Practice gratitude daily.** Begin your day by listing three things you are grateful for, right as you get out of bed. You can simply think about them or take it a step further and write them down in a gratitude journal.

As you move throughout your day, let the people around you know you are grateful to have them in your life. "I'm grateful you were able to be helpful on this team call today." "Thank you so much for bringing me this coffee. I'm grateful for you picking up coffee for me." "I'm really grateful for you taking the time to be so positive today. It means a lot." Maybe you can send three texts out every day at lunch to thank people for the ways they have made your life better. Or just take a few seconds to let the people around you know you appreciate them and why.

Finally, before you go to sleep each night, list three things you are grateful for that day. Once again, write them down if that works best for you. Then observe how different you feel in this more present and positive state as you drift off to sleep. After a week of this gratitude focus, check in with yourself to see what has changed.

The key is to approach the Mindset Habit with a spirit of curiosity, courage, openness, and playfulness. It's often said that by taking generous action, you are aligning yourself with the flow of abundance. As you express more gratitude, you may feel a sense of prosperity in your life.

That's why the Mindset Habit is the first habit you need to make money easy.

YOUR GAME PLAN

Exercise 1: Gratitude Is Free

Gratitude costs you nothing, but it is the core to getting everything you want. The secret is to build a daily gratitude habit. To make it simple, use the following prompts to make a list of the wealth that is already in your life. The more you do this regularly, the more you change the way you see things, and the more likely you are to position yourself to attract wealth.

Use these prompts as daily gratitude starters:

Monday: Something physical that made me feel strong is . . .

Tuesday: Something emotional that made me feel whole is . . .

Wednesday: Something spiritual that made me feel enlightened is . . .

Thursday: Something fun that made me laugh or smile is . . .

Friday: A conversation or interaction I had today that brought me hope is . . .

Saturday: A new thought I had that expanded my thinking is . . .

Sunday: An improved self-belief that opened my eyes to
   possibilities is . . .

   Use these prompts, or others you create for yourself, to express
gratitude every single day. It's free, and it tells the universe you are
ready to receive more.

Exercise 2: Give Away Money Today

This activity is about putting giving into action. Before you begin
the next chapter, give some money away. Don't overcomplicate it.
Make it simple. But be sure to do it. Here's how it might look:

- Think about a cause you care about, find an
  organization working on that cause, and donate money
  online now.

- Think about a friend or acquaintance you know who is
  struggling financially. Send them some money using
  Zelle or Venmo.

- Consider someone you know who is investing in their
  self-development. Reach out and offer to pay for a
  course or training.

- Pay for the person in line behind you at the drive-thru
  or in the coffee shop.

- Pay for someone else who's having lunch in the same
  restaurant you are . . . without their knowing who
  covered the bill.

- Walk up to a stranger in the store and hand them cash.

   It doesn't matter which of these you choose, and feel free to
make up your own; the important thing is to practice generosity
now. And be grateful for whatever you can do.

Exercise 3: Plant a Few Generosity Seeds

Brainstorm a list of long-term "generosity seeds" that you can plant
today. Write a few sentences about what that "tree" will look like in
the years to come. Who will sit under its shade? How will they be
helped? Who do you know who could help you dig? Plant small,
but dream big.

The Seed	The Shade
I'm an entrepreneur who loves to mentor high school students, so I will reach out to our local school and offer to meet with a student once a month to teach them how to leverage their experience to build their own business.	In 10 years, this student will have built upon our time together. They will have founded their own company, and that company is now innovating in ways we don't even know exist today. In turn, they mentor a group of high school girls who want to build their own companies to impact others.

CHAPTER SEVEN

HABIT 2:
THE MAPPING HABIT

Plan Your Life

The summer between my seventh and eighth grade years, my parents sent me off to attend a Christian Science summer camp in Missouri. While there, I came up with a plan I knew would change the trajectory of my life: in the fall I was going to attend a private Christian Science boarding school located a seven-hour drive away from home, and I wouldn't take no for an answer.

One of my older sisters had already gone away to college, and the other would be graduating from high school soon. My brother had recently come home from prison after being locked up for four and a half years. Being so much younger than my siblings, I felt alone. I think most kids go through a season where they feel misunderstood, and I was no exception.

For one thing, there was a lot of tension between my parents. I remember trying to drown out the sounds of their screaming and slamming doors as they fought. It wasn't something my parents set out to cause, but the subconscious way I interpreted my family dynamics contributed to my emotional and mental trauma, confusion, and insecurities. I would count the days until summer camp when I could relax and have fun with other kids my age.

Just like at every other summer camp, we were kept busy with five to ten daily activities. We'd play basketball, go waterskiing, jump into the lake from rope swings, and ride horses—just to name a few. Because the camp was for Christian Scientists, before every activity we'd have five-minute "mets," or metaphysical intention setting. We'd create an intention for how we wanted to live during the next activity from a metaphysical and spiritual perspective by asking ourselves: *What am I looking to create here? How do I want to show up at this moment? What happened to me yesterday that I want to reflect on, discuss, and work through?*

Going through mets every day for those two weeks laid the foundation for helping me become more thoughtful, grounded, and intentional about the way I wanted to show up in my life. These habits and rituals still help me in all kinds of different situations, from giving speeches to professional and personal interactions. When I have a clear dream, vision, or goal in my mind, I'll do whatever I can, in the most authentic way, to achieve it.

I found out that many of my camp friends went to a private school for Christian Scientists in St. Louis, Missouri. I was having a blast with them, and they wholeheartedly accepted me, so I concluded that enrolling in their school was the only way to get my life back on track for the next five years, from eighth grade through high school.

When my parents met me at the airport back home in Columbus, Ohio, the first thing I told them was, "Those kids were positive and inspiring. I want to be around that type of energy. So I want to go to their school in St. Louis, Missouri." My parents immediately responded with all the reasons it couldn't happen—we didn't have the money for private boarding school; they wanted me to stay home with them; I didn't have the grades. But I *knew* it was going to happen.

All summer I hounded them. More importantly, I planned everything I needed to do before the next school year started. I applied to the school. I wrote essays, got letters from my church, and tracked down scholarships and applied for them. I promised my parents I'd work with tutors and do summer school if I had to. And when the time came, they let me go!

Even though the school was strict and the curriculum challenging, the experience there gave me a strong mental foundation. It gave me the secret sauce that helped me in high school and college sports. To this day, I still live with a lot of the practices and teachings from that school on a daily basis. And I've seen some powerful lessons come full circle during different conversations on my show.

I know I wouldn't be where I am today without making that plan and following through on it.

WHY PLANS LACK PROGRESS

Do you make New Year's resolutions? If you do, how many have you kept? Did you know that 23 percent of Americans quit those resolutions by the end of the first week? Another 43 percent quit by the end of January. If you completed a resolution, you're among only 9 percent of the people who follow through on those plans.[1]

We seem to have the same problems making plans with our money. Why is that? Here are some of the issues we seem to struggle with the most:

1. **We lose our motivation.** We all go through different money seasons in life. At one point, I worked jobs solely for the money they provided. I drove trucks, mowed lawns, and even worked as a bouncer at a club. Those jobs had nothing to do with my specific skill sets or interests. I just needed to pay the bills. It's easy to get lost in the routine and lose the motivation to go after something better when you aren't sure how you'd make money in an exciting and even fulfilling way.

2. **We distract ourselves.** Investor and entrepreneur Alex Hormozi made this point to me: Instead of creating plans to decide the next action, a lot of people distract

themselves to avoid having to face reality. Sitting on the couch and bingeing an entire season of a show, playing a video game, or scrolling through social media offers an easily accessible escape. People don't have to think about how much they don't like their jobs or what they might do to improve their situation. But when they do this day after day, nothing changes.

3. **We get overwhelmed by the next level.** It doesn't matter if you're moving from five figures to six, six to seven, or seven to eight. Getting over the hump from one income level to the next can be hard to deal with, both mentally and emotionally. Each time you make it to the next level, your mind has no frame of reference to help you adjust. Instead of following through and leveling up, it can be easy to create excuses and set plans aside to stay in your comfort zone.

4. **We avoid prosperous habits.** Robin Sharma, personal mastery leader and worldwide best-selling author of *The Monk Who Sold His Ferrari* and *The Wealth Money Can't Buy*, shared a powerful concept with me. It's a way of thinking from his book *The Everyday Hero Manifesto*. Instead of staying in a victim mentality where things are just the way they are and you have no control over the outcomes in your life, you can shift into a hero mentality.

   Robin suggests paying close attention to the words we say. Instead of creating a vocabulary filled with negativity, we can change how we speak about our situations. Doing this can bring more opportunities to have more of what we want in life—financially, personally, physically, and professionally.

   Another prosperous habit is to educate yourself by reading books that inspire you and lift you up instead of staring at a screen. Changing your foundational habits can make a huge difference in the quest to change your financial situation.

CREATE YOUR MONEY VISION

A tourist visited a small fishing village. While there, he struck up a conversation with a local fisherman. Admiring the man's small business, the tourist asked, "How long does it take for you to catch the fish?"

The fisherman replied, "Not very long."

"Why don't you stay on the water longer each day so you can catch more fish?"

"The small catches I get each day are sufficient to meet my needs and those of the families in my village."

"What do you do with the rest of your time?"

"We sleep late, we fish some, play with our kids, and take siestas with our wives. In the evenings we go into the village to spend time with our friends, have a few drinks, play the guitar, and sing a few songs. We have a full life."

The tourist interrupted the fisherman. "I have an MBA from Harvard, and I'd love to help you. If you start by fishing longer every day, you can sell the extra fish you catch. Then, with the extra revenue, you can buy a bigger boat."

"That's interesting," replied the fisherman, "then what?"

"With the extra money and the bigger boat, you can buy a second boat and keep working until you have an entire fleet of fishing boats. Then, instead of selling your fish to a middleman, you can negotiate directly with processing plants and maybe even open your own plant. You could then have the resources to move to a big city and direct your huge enterprise from there."

"How long would that take?"

"Oh, maybe twenty to twenty-five years."

Then the fisherman asked, "What would I do after that?"

The tourist happily replied, "You can do some interesting things. When your business is really big, you can start buying and selling stocks to make even more millions."

"Millions? What do I do after I have millions of dollars?"

"That's when you can retire and live in a tiny village near the coast, sleep late, play with your children, catch a few fish, take a siesta with your wife, and spend your evenings drinking and enjoying music with your friends."

The fisherman nodded his head, then replied, "With all due respect, sir, that's exactly what I'm doing right now. I don't see the point in wasting twenty-five years."[2]

I love that simple story because it illustrates a powerful point: You must know what kind of rich life you want before you can plan to live it. And only you can decide for yourself how to define it.

When we aren't clear on our direction, we typically waste time on things that don't support our growth and development or service to others. That's often when anxiety, depression, and stress show up. We begin to ask whether there's something wrong with us. Often it all happens because we didn't put a plan in place to live a richer life.

On the one hand, I see the allure of the fisherman in the village. I've experienced that kind of life at times. It can be fun to take it easy and do the bare minimum. There's joy, fun, and not much stress. If that is your definition of a richer life, then go for it. Grab a pole and find your village.

But although I don't fully agree with the tourist either, I know there are gifts and talents inside you that can make your family, your community, and the world around you a better place. If you never maximize your potential, you'll miss out on a more abundant life that is both deeply fulfilling for you and makes others' lives richer in incredible ways.

I'm not here to make you feel any guilt or shame for whatever way you choose to visualize a rich life. Maybe having a small, simple life with just enough money and spending time with friends and family sounds good to you. Or maybe what you see is working long hours to generate millions of dollars that you can use to create more opportunities for yourself and your family.

My money vision has evolved and changed over the years. For me a rich life includes the ability to expand and grow emotionally, spiritually, and financially. My rich life includes meaningful relationships, a healthy body, financial peace, and spiritual harmony. It also includes the resources my team needs to help reach and impact 100 million people each week to create their own version of a richer life.

Take the time
to understand
what a rich life
means to you.

— Lewis Howes

LOWER YOUR STANDARDS

Once you take the time to understand what a rich life means to you, it's time to do something about it—make some plans and map out how you're going to get there because *if you never map out your future, you'll tend to retrace your past.*

By getting intentional about where you want to go in life, you keep yourself from slipping back into past traps or traumas you once thought were healed. It's time to give yourself permission to pursue plans you may have set aside in the past.

I've challenged my mom to do just that in the last few years. I started by asking her, "What do you really want to do that you've never done before?" She mentioned wanting to travel to Hawaii, so we sat down and made a plan. Two weeks later, she stepped off the plane and breathed in the scent of tropical flowers on the Big Island. Her sense of accomplishment matched the beaming smile on her face.

Since then she's continued to try new things. She took new dance classes, joined knitting clubs and a church choir, and tried different physical activities. She's spending more quality time with friends and family. I love to see her youthful energy shining through as she goes on new adventures. My advice to her now is, "Keep doing it!" The more she does the things that make her excited and joyful, the easier it is for her to create the next set of plans. I'm proud of her for taking the first step and then flowing with the momentum that came from taking action.

Kelly McGonigal, neuroscientist and author of *The Willpower Instinct,* defines *willpower* as "the ability to make choices that are consistent with your most important goals and values even when some part of you doesn't want to."[3] She says willpower isn't about forcing yourself to always do one thing or suppressing your urge to do something else. It's more about getting really clear on aligning your goals with who you are and where you want to go and then playing with some neurological tools to help you achieve what you want.

If you never
map out
your future,
you'll tend
to retrace
your past.

— Lewis Howes

One such tool is lowering your standards. Yes, you read that right. It may initially sound like you're giving up and settling for something less than your desired outcome, but it's really a great first step toward getting exactly what you want in the long run. For example, maybe you've been researching how to start investing or pay off debt. Instead of trying to change everything overnight, start with one small, consistent action you can take that will move you in the right direction. As you achieve that one thing over and over, you create momentum. Your sense of pride starts to kick in as you feel grateful that you're accomplishing something. It helps you create an environment that supports your goal, even when you're having a bad day.

The cool thing about this technique is that the people around you will start to notice what you're doing. Before you know it, you will be inspiring them to create their own money vision and take their first small steps too. Kelly explained to me how a component of willpower is a biological mind/body response:

> In contrast to the fight-or-flight instinct, we have one that slows us down called pause and plan. It first requires that you know what your goals are.
>
> When your mind recognizes you're in a moment that is pulling you away from your goals and commitments—you're tempted, distracted, or self-doubting—pause and plan kicks in. It decelerates your heart rate, increases your focus, and activates areas of your brain that help you remember your goals and your values.[4]

Getting clear on your money vision is the first step to strengthening the pause-and-plan instinct, helping you see distractions as threats to fulfilling those goals. As this instinct grows stronger, it becomes easier to see the things that keep you from meeting your daily goal, and it helps you get back on track in a more productive way.

YOUR RICH YEAR

I really like a concept I heard from Bill Perkins, author of *Die with Zero*. He calls it *memory dividends*. He encourages people to spend their money in the seasons of life when they can get the most fulfillment out of these experiences, as opposed to waiting later in life. A lot of people tend to put off using money to make memories until they're older, only to discover they simply can't physically do what they need to do to experience those things as they age.

For example, I heard of a younger couple who had visited Greece. They were getting ready to climb the stairs to see one of the many ancient wonders there when an elderly couple asked if the younger couple would take a picture on their behalf when they reached the top of the stairs. Unfortunately, the older couple had always wanted to visit the site, but by the time they actually arrived, they simply couldn't make it up the stairs.

That's why Perkins talks about investing in experiences that give you rich memories to lean in to as you go through life, thus producing the memory dividends that compound over time. With this approach, you map your life to spend your money strategically to create experiences with a time value. These experiences will pay dividends through photos, videos, adventures, random human encounters, beautiful moments, and memories that you will treasure later as you live your richer life.

My friend Jesse Itzler, an Emmy award–winning artist, *New York Times* best-selling author, part-owner of the Atlanta Hawks, and ultramarathon runner, talks about doing this for your entire life over the course of a year. He even offers a helpful "Big Ass Calendar" you can post on your wall to bring your plan to life. In this process, he shows you how to map out the big moments, trips, or experiences you want to take on for the year—you write them down someplace where you can see them on a big calendar that you hang on your wall and then fill in the rest of life's responsibilities for that year around them.

If that's helpful for you, I suggest you do it. But what if you could create your perfect-year plan based on the signature experiences you want to invest in? Even if everything else falls apart but you are able to create those core memories, what experiences and adventures would enable you to say you had a rich year because they added so much good to your life?

Imagine if you used your money to create these signature experiences, maybe one every quarter or every two months. These four to six experiences would go on your calendar first before you let all the other life stuff fill in around them. Then you could develop a financial plan to create those memory dividends Bill Perkins describes.

Now imagine if you did this for 40 years. You could have at least 240 unique trips, moments, and experiences, each with a range of other experiences attached to it, for thousands of memories throughout your lifetime.

You don't have to map out all those experiences for the next 40 years or even the next 5 years. Some people do try to map out their entire lives and all the decisions to be made, but I've never found life to be predictable enough to make that worthwhile. Even a few years out can be a challenge at times. Just focus on the next 12 months. What would that year look like? Would it be the richest year of your life, regardless of how much you spend on those experiences?

If thinking even a year in advance is too much planning for you right now, start with one day. What would a rich day in your life look like if you didn't spend a dime? The richest moments in life don't come from spending money but rather from experiencing moments of connection, intimacy, fun, or realization. They come from overcoming challenges together with someone you care about—and they don't necessarily require money. Would your rich day include taking time to go to the gym, picking your child up from school, or having a deeper conversation with someone you love? Money can give you more options, but if you don't have a rich inner life and rich relationships already, it will simply magnify your misery.

What would
a rich day in
your life look
like if you didn't
spend a dime?

— Lewis Howes

In fact, since money doesn't guarantee happiness, what would a rich day look like for you if you *didn't* spend any money?

- Are you alone or with others?
- If you're with others, who are you spending time with?
- What activities are you doing?
- Which hobbies, passions, or unique experiences are you engaging in?
- What emotions are you feeling?
- What do you want to feel grateful for on this rich day?

Now consider what that rich day might look like if you *did* spend money. Would you take a friend to lunch? Attend a special event where you can make memories with others? Would you travel to the beach, hike in the mountains, visit a theme park, or throw a party for a good friend? What might your ideal rich day look and feel like?

That's not to say either day is better, with or without money. But when we disconnect the idea of living a richer life from spending money, we open new possibilities. Then we can reintegrate both approaches to create our ideal richer-life day.

With practice, you can make this more of a life posture. As you roll out of bed in the morning, you might think, *What one thing can I do today to upgrade an experience, relationship, or interaction to make it richer?* If you've already started practicing the Mindset Habit, you will already be in a grateful spiritual posture as your feet hit the floor to start the day.

But no matter what you do, if you haven't healed your relationship with money and done the work on your inner self, all the money in the world won't produce a richer life for you. You first need to have a rich relationship with yourself, doing that healing work with yourself and others, and doing that healing work with money. Only then can you flourish and enjoy a feeling of abundance.

A rich life is not a self-centered life but one focused on the memories and moments with other people.

MAP YOUR NEXT STEPS

Patrick Bet-David, author of the number-one *Wall Street Journal* bestseller *Your Next Five Moves*, told me about the power of sequencing as a key to planning success. For example, two people may have the same vision of what they want to do in life. Let's say they both want careers as professional football players. There are countless steps and options to reach that level of success, but the person who chooses the better sequencing of them will inevitably get there faster, while the other person with less-efficient sequencing may never get there at all.

Patrick experienced this sequencing power firsthand when his life started falling apart around him. When he was 26 years old, his girlfriend broke up with him because he loved his business more than her. After that, he got a message from his mom asking him what had happened to her little son who used to love his mother. *Then* he read an email from a client who was supposed to pay him $15,000 saying they were backing out of the deal. *And all of this happened before 6:10 A.M.* Here's how he described it:

> "I had no idea what to do in that moment. All I thought about was, *What are my next five moves? What do I need to do next?* From that moment on, everything I did with business came down to my next five moves."[5]

So often we say we want to make more money or we're frustrated about not having enough. We say we want *more* without a clear vision about exactly *how much* we want or *when* we want it.

When I was broke on my sister's couch, this is the vision I wrote for myself: *I will make $5,000 from a speech in nine months.* I signed the piece of paper, framed it, and mounted it on the wall. It was there staring me in the face every day. Anytime I felt distracted, there my intention was, waiting for me to act.

Please understand that I didn't achieve that first goal just by writing it down and thinking about it. I had to overcome all the excuses I was making about why I didn't have money. I had to act on a daily basis. Most of my weeks were focused on practicing public speaking, giving free speeches online and in person, building my brand and relationships, and finding ways to get in the right rooms. And wouldn't you know it—just before the nine-month mark, I made my first $5,000. It happened even though I'd never made money on speaking before that day and could hardly stand in front of a group without trembling!

Believe me, if I could do it back then, it is possible for you too. Whether you're making no money right now or already generating a seven-figure income, you need to get absolutely clear on what you want your Money Story to be in the future. Money isn't going to show up in your lap while you sit on the couch. If you're struggling to get to the next level financially, try asking yourself these questions:

1. How much do I want to make?
2. Why do I want to make that?
3. What will I do with the money when I make it?
4. When do I want to make it?
5. What fears do I need to overcome?
6. What do I need to learn?
7. With whom do I need to connect?
8. What skills do I need to master?
9. What actions do I need to take?

You've probably heard the saying "You are what you eat." But did you know that your life is shaped by your internal monologue? So it's more accurate to say, "You are what you think." What you think, focus on, and tell yourself will determine your direction— for your good or not.

That's why it's crucial to have a Meaningful Mission. Without a mission or purpose in life, you're like a person taking a trip without a destination, plan, or road map. Spontaneity and spur-of-the-moment decisions can be fun and add excitement to life, but you need direction or you'll never get anywhere.

For eight years, I dreamed of being a *New York Times* best-selling author. Almost every night, I focused on what it would look like to walk into a bookstore and see my book on the front shelf with *"New York Times* bestseller" next to my name.

Achieving my dream wouldn't have happened without the goal I visualized and worked toward one step at a time. Now that I've written my second *New York Times* bestseller, I understand the importance of visualizing when it comes to goal setting and taking massive action.

KNOW THE NUMBERS

Once you understand the specific Money Story you want to live, it's time to get familiar with the numbers. Whether you want to make your first $1,000 or six, seven, or even eight figures in the next year, you need to know what it will take to get you there.

Let's break it down into some practical steps you can take right now:

1. **Envision your money goal.** Start by writing down the exact amount of money that you want to accumulate. Make this number big enough that it feels uncomfortable, maybe even laughable, when you consider where you are now. Think about the Money Story you want to live and how much it will take for you to achieve it.

2. **Do the math.** Get out your calculator, a piece of paper, and a pencil. Let's say you want $100,000 in a year. Figure out how much you need to make in a month, a week, and a day, along with your hourly rate.

   - *Month:* Divide your yearly goal ($100,000) by 12 months in the year. You will need to make $8,333 each month.

   - *Week:* Divide your yearly goal ($100,000) by 48 weeks in a year, assuming you take some time off. You will need to make $2,083 per week.

   - *Day:* Divide your weekly goal ($2,083) by 5 days in a week, assuming you take weekends off. You will need to make $417 per day to hit your $100,000 yearly goal.

- *Hour:* Divide your daily goal ($400) by 8 since the average working day is 8 hours long. You will need to make about $52/hour to hit your $100,000 yearly goal.

3. **Brainstorm ideas to create income.** Now it's time to maximize your income. Keep in mind that it's important to add value to the world. If you can't do that, it will be difficult to make money consistently.

   - What knowledge, special skills, or talents do you have that you could teach someone else?

   - What services can you share and be paid for that will be of value?

   - Can you consult with someone about something?

   - Is there a product you could create and sell?

   - Is there a service you could provide?

   - How much have people paid you, or would be willing to pay you, for these things?

4. **Create your plan.** Use your list of valuable services and products and do the math again. If you have an hourly rate, how many hours will you need to work to achieve your goal? If you have a product or service to sell, how many of these would you need to sell?

   Make a plan based on these numbers. If the numbers aren't adding up, look at what you can do. Find a mentor to support you as you work on leveling up. Invest in yourself and gain the skills to create the value that will, in turn, create income.

5. **Just do it!** After you have your plan, it's time to go for it. Create momentum by taking intentional action every day. Sure, there will be setbacks, but you must keep pushing toward your goals. When you stay consistent and keep pushing yourself forward, you will surprise yourself as you start writing a new Money Story.

It feels great to have a plan, doesn't it? But your plan can't become a reality if you don't believe you're worthy of it. Up next, we'll work on the importance of understanding the value you bring to the world and how to package it to create maximum impact.

YOUR GAME PLAN

Exercise 1: Live A Richer Day; Build a Richer Life

The richest days of your life rarely involve money. Rather, they involve experiences, conversations, relationships, and memories. This exercise will help you create a chart to think about past rich experiences and challenge you to create a richer day without spending money.

In the left column of the chart, reflect on your past. What were some of your best days? What made them great? What did you gain for free? Who was with you? In what ways were you able to creatively make magic happen?

In the middle column, reflect on what you currently have at your disposal. This could be a great family who makes you feel loved. It could be a friend who knows how to make you laugh or pushes you just to the edge of your comfort zone. It could be a local park with a beautiful walking trail. It could be a blank journal and a pen. Whatever you presently have that fills you with joy, add it to the list.

In the far-right column, begin to write out a scenario in which you can have your richest day yet. Use memories from the past and present resources to create this day. Describe it in detail. Who is with you? What are you doing? How do you feel? Abundant, fulfilled, positive, confident? Why do you feel rich? How will these memories stick with you for the rest of your life?

Repeat this process any time you need a reminder of what richness truly is. When you stack rich days, you build a rich life. This compounding builds those memory dividends that make life amazing.

My Past Riches	My Present Resources	My Richest Day
Example: When my sister and I played games together on our front porch after school every day when I was in fifth grade	*Example:* My spouse, whom I adore	*Example:* I'm with my wife and all three of my kids, and we're enjoying a week-long family vacation in the South Carolina Lowcountry

Exercise 2: Create Your Money Moves Map

Think about a goal you've had for making money. Write it in a simple sentence, like the example from this chapter about making $5,000 from a speaking engagement. If you have never articulated this goal, use these seven questions to build your statement:

1. How much do I want to make?

2. When do I want to make it?

3. What fears do I need to overcome?

4. What do I need to learn?

5. With whom do I need to connect?

6. What skills do I need to master?

7. What actions do I need to take?

Now map out the next five moves you can make to move the needle. Keep them simple and actionable. Add a completion target date beside each move, and then put your Money Moves Map in a place where you can see it. When you finish one move, add a new one to the list. Keep these next five moves in front of you as a way to break big things into small steps and stay accountable.

What are your next five moves? What's your targeted completion date?

1. _____

2. _____

3. _____

4. _____

5. _____

CHAPTER EIGHT

HABIT 3: THE MONETIZING HABIT

Appreciate Your Value

The amount of money you make is directly related to the amount of value you bring to others *and* your ability to package and sell that value. I call it the Monetizing Habit. It's both simple and potentially challenging.

Even after people adopt the first habit of making money with a grateful mindset, and after they embrace the second habit of mapping their plan, they tend to stumble on this third one. I think it's because it truly puts to the test how much you appreciate your own value. Because the truth is this: if you don't value yourself—your talents, time, skills, abilities, and ultimately your worth—you'll always struggle to figure out how to turn that value into money.

Allyson Felix did just that. To date, she is the most decorated track-and-field athlete in history with an astounding 31 Olympic and World Championship medals. But even she had to face the long-standing culture in track-and-field of unfair treatment with regard to pregnancy and motherhood. Allyson saw her teammates struggling to start their families as they hid their pregnancies to keep their sponsorship contracts. She didn't see many examples of mothers dominating in the sport—not because the women weren't capable but because the support to make it possible didn't exist.

When she decided to start a family at age 33, she was scared about how contract negotiations would go with Nike, her then sponsor. Even before she became pregnant, they had reduced her contract by 30 percent simply because she was older. So she chose to do what so many other women in the sport had done—hide her pregnancy for as long as she could. From training at night to wearing baggy clothes and hardly leaving the house, she ping-ponged between being excited to have her first child and worrying about losing her sponsorship.

Finally, knowing Nike was likely to pursue younger athletes anyway, she decided she had nothing to lose. She chose to shift the negotiations. Rather than focus on the money she would make with her next contract, she fought to secure maternal protections in contracts, not only for herself but also for all female athletes whom Nike would sponsor in the future.

Nike agreed to those requests—but only for her, not as a precedent for future sponsorships. And Allyson made the difficult decision to walk away.

Notice what had happened: Allyson had approached the problem with a generous mindset and Meaningful Mission (Habit 1) by seeking to give value to other women. Then she mapped a plan (Habit 2) to deliver that value. Then she came to more fully appreciate the value she could give to the world (Habit 3), and it was about a purpose greater than winning more medals.

Allyson then met with Athleta, a company with whose vision she aligned. They became her apparel sponsor. However, as Allyson headed toward the next Olympics, she realized she had no sponsored shoes to wear. So she and her brother, who was also her manager, decided to create their own. As they began researching the shoe-creation process, Allyson was shocked to discover that women's athletic shoes were made from a cast based on a man's foot.

The two of them created a new brand of shoes designed specifically for women. They even established a maternity returns policy since women's feet often increase by half a size or more during pregnancy, and the sizing changes tend to be permanent.

Instead of hoping companies would see her value, Allyson flipped the script and chose to see and appreciate her own unique value. Once she learned how to communicate that value, she was, pun intended, off to the races. And the same can be true for you.

You may not be an Olympic athlete, but we all experience identity shifts throughout our lives. Who am I apart from what I do? Who am I if my relationship status changes? Am I still valuable without this career I've worked so hard for? And at the root of so many of those questions during those seasons: *Am I still valuable?*

GET DIFFERENT

You *are* worthy. You *are* loved. You *are* enough. But sometimes it takes some work to get to the place where *you* can believe that to be true and identify ways you can exchange that unique value for money.

This crucial lesson took me a while to grasp, but once I did, I never undersold myself again. Early in my career, after I was looking for what might be next after success with LinkedIn training, I invested time, energy, and money into my unique personal brand. I wasn't necessarily smarter, more talented, or more experienced than anyone else in my field. But I knew I had a different perspective.

I had that confirmed when friend and speaker Sally Hogshead told me, "Different is better than better." She was so right. I knew that if I could look unique, I would stand out. I started researching and studying from experts on how to become a master of personal branding. I knew I wouldn't be smarter or more talented than most in my industry, so I wanted to find a different way to package and promote myself to build my business. Not try to "beat" others but rather try to stand out as myself. I invested in great photographs and designers to help create an elevated digital look beyond what others were doing at the time.

In fact, the concept for *The School of Greatness* show came out of a desire to present content in a different way that would allow me to do what I loved while also helping people. As I sat at a stand-still in Los Angeles traffic one day thinking about my next moves, podcasting came to mind. In that moment, I called two people I knew who had podcasts. They said they were having a blast and connecting with new audiences in fresh ways because of it. That sounded different to me. And this was in 2012, when no one knew what podcasting was!

All around me, people honked and yelled, but no one really moved forward. We were all stuck. *Hmmm*, I thought. *Maybe I could help people get unstuck by helping them learn—and improve my own life in the process.* At that moment, *The School of Greatness* show was born. Podcasting allowed me to deliver value based on my own unique strengths of asking questions and interviewing people—all while advancing my Meaningful Mission of helping others improve their lives.

As time went on, I began thinking about ways to grow and scale that value to my audience. When we first launched Greatness Media, if we wanted to make more money, I had to be involved in some way. I spoke at the event. I coached a client. I led the digital strategy. We did well, but it was exhausting and limited the impact we could make.

Then I shifted our focus as a company to create scalable products and services that could make money without my constant direct involvement. For a season, we offered membership and mastermind programs to reach more people. Now we invest more into our reach through one of our media outlets and use dynamic advertising on the show, so we don't have to rely on my availability to sell other products all the time. Meanwhile, our evergreen content continues to drive sales and leads. Being able to scale our value allows us to keep growing, whether I'm asleep, awake, traveling, at the gym, or taking a day off.

As Greatness Media continues to grow, we keep exploring and adding new revenue streams that don't depend entirely on me. It hasn't happened all at once. I've tried and failed here and there, but through it all, I've learned a lot about how to package my unique value to the world.

People tend to value us only as much as we value ourselves.

— Lewis Howes

People tend to value us only as much as we value ourselves. If we think and act as though we are worth little, others will treat us as being worth little. But when you know your value and have confidence in sharing that value with the world, you won't sell yourself short in any area of your life.

So how much do you think you are worth? What can you offer that will make an impact? What problems can you solve? How can you uniquely serve others? Most importantly, how much are people willing and able to pay for what you offer? What skills do you have that could produce revenue streams? Look at your current situation to figure out what the next best revenue stream could be and start there. You don't have to overwhelm yourself with five new directions today. Start with one skill and commit to following the process to make it great.

THE VALUE APPRECIATION LADDER

Think of this process as a ladder to be climbed. Once your plan is mapped in Habit 2, you know what wall you want to climb. According to your plan, before you start climbing, you'll first want to be sure the ladder is leaning against the right wall. But when you do get ready to make money by leveraging your unique value, I suggest you think about it in terms of the Value Appreciation Ladder.

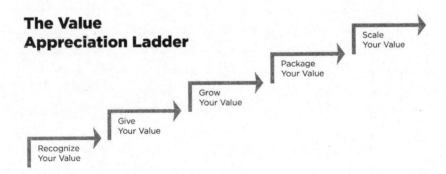

The Value Appreciation Ladder

Recognize Your Value → Give Your Value → Grow Your Value → Package Your Value → Scale Your Value

This ladder illustrates what I mean when I say you need to appreciate your value. All five of these steps are taken over time as part of the Monetizing Habit. Let's unpack more about each one.

Step 1: Recognize Your Value. You can't appreciate what you don't know. That's why you must first see your own unique value and come to "monetize" it internally before you try to monetize it to the world. It might be surprising to hear, but you don't need money to feel rich. In fact, you can feel rich simply by learning to value who you are becoming at every rung of the ladder.

I know: On the one hand, this is a book about making money. But if you want to live a richer life, you must always be creating richness and abundance within, even when your value or the value of what matters most to you is not attached to money. Now I'm not saying you should ignore money or try to be poor in order to be happy; however, first focus throughout your journey on what makes you rich in heart and appreciate how much you have grown at each level as you make your way up the ladder.

With that in mind, the first obstacle to overcome on this first step is the belief that your skills aren't valuable. Most people have already developed incredibly useful skills, even if they haven't learned how to apply them to making money. Perhaps you have been successful in one industry and haven't yet realized those skills are transferable to other areas. Or perhaps technology has shifted and given you the opportunity to repurpose your talents in some pretty cool ways.

But if you think you don't have any unique talents or skills, I guarantee that the Money Story you are telling yourself is not true. When I first started, I didn't think building relationships and networking were valuable skills. They were just something I naturally did. I hadn't yet realized that these were competencies people would be willing to hire and pay me for.

Once I did, I started thinking outside the box. I created my own lane. I intentionally worked to grow my value in a way that made me money. I was able to creatively monetize my skills, even though initially there were no job opportunities for making introductions.

To help identify what those skills might be for you, consider these questions:

- What natural-born talents have others recognized in me?

- What do I do naturally and easily that others seem to have appreciated?

- What parts of my personality have helped open new doors?

- What experiences have taught me something useful I didn't know before?

- In what settings do I find myself excelling?

- What problems do I think I can uniquely help solve?

- What am I good at (even if I don't yet see how to monetize it)?

- What do I love and appreciate about myself and the value I bring to the world?

Step 2: Give Your Value. Living a rich life isn't *just* about you feeling rich on the inside. The next step is to use your skills to help others live a richer life in a unique way. Clearly, this step connects directly to the Mindset Habit. Not only does Habit 1 help you avoid a scarcity mentality, but being generous with your talents also helps you take the next step up the ladder by giving you a low-risk opportunity to hone your skills.

When I was just getting started with my business, I would often find ways to add value to people for free. *Here's something I've learned,* I thought. *How can I use this to help someone else?* I was doing it in service of helping people live richer lives, but it also enriched my life by giving me valuable experience. And if I got it wrong, I had nothing to lose. How could someone complain when I wasn't charging them anything for the help?

Your value
appreciates
every time
you use your
skill set to help
someone else.

— Lewis Howes

Your value appreciates every time you use your skill set to help someone else. I saw this happen right away after I helped someone and he said, "What you've taught me is going to help me grow my business in a big way. Here's a hundred dollars." Now the connection isn't always so direct, but when you give your value to others, you'll eventually see money or something else of value flowing back to you.

The benefits of serving people can extend beyond the immediate outcomes too. Every time you serve a client, help a customer, or do pro bono work, there's a ripple effect. As more people come to know about you and your work, your gift of value can come back to you in unforeseen positive ways.

Step 3: Grow Your Value. As you learn to recognize your value and give it to others, you can't settle for the second rung on the ladder. You must keep growing your potential value. A few obvious ways to increase your skills and hone your talents are via schooling, apprenticeships, or other experiences.

But one-time, formal training is not enough. You need to maintain an awareness of what is happening in the marketplace. Industries shift, technologies evolve, and business needs change from season to season. When that happens, certain skills become more or less valuable. Staying on top of these changes helps you know whether you need to start learning new skills or reorienting your current skills in a new direction.

You want to grow in a way that increases your value over time. Some people can get good at one skill and focus on that skill for a long time to become experts. For example, a computer programmer might zero in on coding skills and spend less energy developing other competencies. When they do, their main skill can appreciate. That kind of expert talent is scarce. As Rory Vaden, *New York Times* best-selling author, entrepreneur, and co-founder of the Brand Builders Group, told me, "When you're difficult to replace, your stock goes up."

But there is a trade-off to becoming the "one-trick pony." Even if that is a viable option in your field, you never know how future changes such as artificial intelligence might test your ability to remain relevant. And if you don't continuously expand your market awareness and knowledge and continue to grow your skills in those directions, you'll end up developing a skill set that the market no longer values.

Step 4: Package Your Value. A popular myth says that if you provide a great product or service, you will succeed. But the truth is, while you may have some success with it, you'll achieve nowhere near the success you could have unless you learn to package it well.

This next step on the Value Appreciation Ladder should almost be the length of several steps because doing it will move rapidly and separate you from nearly everyone else. Serving others can help with this packaging in many ways, but if you want to make the most of your value, you must master the art of marketing yourself too. You could be the best guitarist, designer, or writer in the world, but if no one knows your value because you haven't packaged it well, your valuable assets won't be seen by many people.

Packaging your value has everything to do with building a personal brand and leveraging your relationships to tell your story well. It's about figuring out what you do best and then conveying that to your intended audience in a way that illustrates your value. You want them to not only understand what you do but also want to give you money for doing it. This will mean putting yourself in uncomfortable situations. People might reject you, not hire you, or not purchase what you offer. Just remember that failure is feedback and is the means for growth.

As your skills improve, you will need to find people who are willing and able to pay you for those skills. Ask yourself these questions to find your customers:

- Who are the people who will recognize the value of what I'm offering?
- Who will be willing and able to pay for it?
- Can they clearly understand what I'm offering?

- Am I offering it in such a way that makes it easy for them to buy?

- Who are the people whose lives will be enriched by the skills I have to offer?

- Who will have the most to gain from my value *and* has the ability to pay me for it?

Everyone has valuable skills. But not everyone knows how to package them in a way that stands out. In short, a great way to make yourself recession proof is to level up your personal brand.

Step 5: Scale Your Value. Once you figure out how to package your value, you will be positioned to scale what you offer to make more money easily. I'll talk more about how to scale in Habit 6: The Mobility Habit. For now, just know that you can't get there until you take the first four steps to set yourself up to live a richer life—and make more money doing it.

One thing to note about the process of monetizing your value is that it's not just a one-and-done. It's a muscle you develop that requires continual upkeep. Just like an athlete in training, you must put in the reps, push past resistance, and push yourself to do things you couldn't have done before. To effectively monetize in the long run, you often have to start climbing again from the bottom up. But each time you do, you get better at it.

Keep in mind that rather than *moving on* from a step, you *build up* from it. As you acquire each new skill and overcome each obstacle, you acquire competence, which gives you the confidence to do more with the skills you already have. This lets you scale your personal brand more and more as you go.

Don't forget to keep internally "monetizing" your value at every step. Look back often to appreciate where you are now compared to where you were. This helps you steer clear of the comparison trap so you can grow from an authentic mindset of abundance for all.

A few words of caution and clarity. First, don't wait until you feel like everything looks perfect before you start giving your value.

So many people are held back by trying to get the perfect website, logo, or product before they begin. Instead just find someone to serve with your skills. Then move on to find the client or customer who is willing to exchange what you have to offer for money. Show them your value, transform it into real results, and you're taking significant steps toward monetizing your skills.

Second, know that people are wired differently. Not everyone will fit into the same box. Some may want to pursue a cause they care about and volunteer while working elsewhere. Some may want to find a company with a mission that excites them and lets them use their talents for that mission. Still others may want to be entrepreneurs and package value in a product or service that serves others.

If you think you may want to do something entrepreneurial but are afraid of going at it on your own, ask yourself *why* you really want to do it. Do you fear you may regret not doing it? If you don't have a compelling *why* to fuel you, is there a company you can work for, learn from, and develop skills with—while getting paid?

No two stories are the same, so do a heart check. Figure out what works for you in your current season and with the Money Story you want to live.

REDEFINING GOLD

The thing that stops most people from appreciating their value is quite simple: fear. As a high-level athlete, I experienced the fear of failure on a regular basis. It's a natural fear. Of course, no one wants to fail. But we often wrongly assume that the satisfaction and fulfillment we desire can only come from a win.

I was surprised to find that even when I won, I would often still criticize myself for what I could have done better. The satisfaction just wasn't there. The victory felt hollow and empty. It was only when I was able to adopt a growth mindset instead of a mindset of perfectionism that I realized the process could be as beneficial and satisfying as the outcome.

When I was playing on the men's USA Team Handball national team, our goal was to go to the Olympics. We worked for eight years toward that goal and never made it. But who did I become over those eight years? That's the prize. During that time, I gained discipline and the ability to set goals and work hard to achieve them. Those skills have helped me become a better person and a better businessperson. Even if you don't meet your goals, the process is worth it. (But yes, I still love winning!)

As Allyson Felix says, "Success doesn't always mean the gold medal. You can do a lot of work along the way, and you can be successful without having the thing that is typically defined as being the ultimate."[1] That is so true.

Rachel Rodgers, who is a wildly successful business owner by any measure today, applied to 90 different judges for clerkships and several law firms only to receive rejection after rejection. It was during the 2008 recession when the market was highly competitive and few people were being hired, and the reality was she wasn't at the top of her class. Although it was a stressful time, when Rachel looked back on it, she called it an amazing learning and growth experience: "Being able to endure rejection and not fall apart from it is one of the best skills in the world."[2]

You don't need to let fear stop you from sharing your value with the world. You can and will recover from failure and rejection. You can learn from it and use what you learn to build your confidence to try again. Sometimes all you need to ensure your value continues to appreciate is a firm belief in yourself, a belief that you can overcome whatever obstacle life throws at you.

Self-doubt is the killer of dreams. So how can you build your confidence as you travel the journey to becoming the person you're meant to be? The only thing standing between you and your goals is *you*! That's right: it's not the lack of time or money, and it's not the people in your life—it's you.

Curate the messages you take in, including from yourself. Sometimes there are inner voices that tell you things like, *I don't deserve it* or, *I can't do that*. Katy Milkman at the Wharton School calls these "internal barriers." They're based on either past experiences or just fear of failure in general.

Self-doubt is the killer of dreams.

— Lewis Howes

Luckily, there's a way to overcome these barriers, and the process starts with taking small steps. First you need to believe that you can overcome any barrier. This growth mindset and internal identity belief are critical in navigating the ebbs and flows of life. The placebo effect is not just something you experience in the medical world—what you believe about yourself and your abilities affects your everyday reality.

What you believe about yourself has a lot to do with who you surround yourself with. To create positive change and build confidence, Katy suggests finding someone or a group of people who can help you in a number of ways. You need people who will give you positive feedback, create a solid social structure around you, allow you to support one another as a team, and provide opportunities for you to both be mentored and mentor others.

Even when you lack confidence, there is always someone who knows less than you do. Helping others get to where you are is a confidence booster. You realize you do have what it takes to move forward toward your goals and help others along the way.

There are several ways you can strengthen your self-worth, but it's a step-by-step process. I don't know anything great that was built in a day. A few ways you can strengthen your self-worth might include:

- Reading self-improvement books
- Participating in skill-building workshops
- Getting life or mindset coaching
- Meditating daily
- Going to therapy
- Finding guiding mentors
- Developing solid relationships with good people
- Practicing positive self-talk
- Doing something you can master

If you struggle with self-worth, consider picking one or two of these techniques. Set a deadline, and possibly even give yourself an incentive to see it through. You'll be amazed to see how your ability to appreciate your own value is boosted by intentionally strengthening your sense of self-worth.

Because here's the deal: Your value starts with how you see you. No matter what, you've got to be willing to act to gain confidence. There is no better investment you can make than in your self-worth. As the anonymous saying goes, "When you learn how much you're worth, you'll stop giving people discounts." (Or you will stop letting people discount you.)

I would add to that: you'll finally start valuing yourself for the valuable person you are.

YOUR GAME PLAN

Exercise 1: What's Easy for Me That's Hard for Someone Else?

We each have talents, gifts, and abilities that are easy for us. So easy, in fact, that we often forget they are valuable assets. For this exercise it's time to brag again and map out what's easy for you. Use the prompts below to get started.

- What can you do that is so engaging you lose yourself in it for hours, like you did when you played as a child?

- What is one complicated thing you know so well that you could do it blindfolded? Is it writing a story, baking a cheesecake, fixing a faulty fill valve, or something else?

- When people ask you for help, what are they most likely to want you to do?

- What do you love doing so much that you've developed a personal tool kit for completing those projects?

- What shortcuts or tips do you find yourself offering others who are working in the same areas that interest you?

What's easy for you is probably hard for someone else. And that someone else is very likely happy to pay you to help them make their life easier. When you see your abilities written out in black and white, it helps you elevate and assign your value and strengthen your Monetizing Habit.

Exercise 2: Take One Uncomfortable Step Forward

The greatest ideas in the world earn zero dollars until they are taken on an uncomfortable journey forward. The first step is to identify your offer and where you can provide the greatest value. You can do that by pairing your answers from Exercise 1 with the answers to these questions:

- Which people will recognize the value of what you're offering?

- Are you reasonably sure they will be willing and able to pay for it?

- Is your offer clear and easy to understand?

When the alignment of these answers is clear, you are ready to take a potentially uncomfortable step forward. It may be asking people to see if they would pay for your service, invest in your Kickstarter, listen to your pitch, or give you feedback on your offer.

Now let's brainstorm a list of people you think might be willing to invest in you.

1. _____

2. _____

3. _____

4. _____

5. _____

6. _____

7. _____

8. _____

9. _____

10. _____

One thing to remember: If you've done the work of determining what you bring to the table and you've identified people you know who would truly benefit from your offer, this step won't feel uncomfortable for long. It will feel empowering! Be courageous and put yourself out there.

CHAPTER NINE

HABIT 4: THE MASTERMIND HABIT

Find Your Influential Relationships

At one point, I thought pro football would be my future path to making money. But after I underwent surgery after breaking my wrist in a game, I was forced to adapt. That injury gave me the life I have today. It also taught me many lessons, though not in the way you might expect.

If you've ever worn a cast, then you know how gross they can get. To help my wrist heal, I wore a cast from my hand to my shoulder for six months. There was no way to clean it. The longer I wore it, the dirtier and smellier it got—it was absolutely disgusting.

Whenever it so much as grazed another part of my body, its rough texture left scratches. It drove me nuts. I had to pretty much perform acrobatics just to get into any long-sleeved shirts or hoodies. I knew the cast was there to protect my injured arm, but I came to see it as a necessary evil to be endured.

During that time Amazon and eBay were taking off, and I became fascinated with discovering how other people were able to build businesses from an idea and then market a product online. What was more astonishing was that people were willing to pay money for some of these wild ideas. During Christmas in 2007, I was gifted a book. Little did I know that the book would open my mind to even more possibilities. That book was *The 4-Hour Workweek* by Timothy Ferriss.

It was having to deal with my cast problem that led to my first product idea, and Tim's book led me to a website where I found a business that could help me create my product.

I had somehow managed to save $70 and used all of it to build a prototype. I needed to create a stand-alone sleeve with a thumb hole. It had to be long enough to cover my entire cast and wide enough to fit snugly without sliding around or making it difficult to pull on. I wanted the material to be soft, like a sweatband, and have two layers of material. I sent the company my product design, wired them the money, and waited for six weeks for my prototype to be shipped.

When the samples arrived, I tore into the packaging and slid the first one over my cast. It was exactly what I wanted! I had a clean and soft sleeve to cover my nasty cast, and I remember thinking, *I might actually be able to sell this!* A friend happened to know an inventor near me in Columbus, Ohio. She made the introductions, and a week and a half later, I wore my invention to our first meeting.

This inventor was a master at building products and licensing them—he had all the experience and expertise I was looking for. He offered to help me with my invention if I interned with him for six months. I happily agreed. I didn't make a ton of money interning, but he taught me everything from graphic design to sales and marketing. A portion of my "payment" was having the opportunity to go for an hour-long walk with him once a week and ask him anything. I even got to be a fly on the wall during his team meetings and learned a lot from just listening. I was consuming information in huge gulps, taking in everything I possibly could.

We went to trade shows together, where I learned about building relationships with vendors. We talked about packaging, how to name products—all kinds of stuff that formed the basis of what I do today.

That experience showed me the power of connections in acquiring the knowledge and expertise I needed to succeed. It also set me on the course to write this book because that mentor was Chris Hawker, the same guy who told me those powerful words: *Money comes to you when you are ready for it.*

Nothing has made a bigger difference in my career and personal growth than developing authentic connections with people who were a few (or even many) steps ahead of me. You could call them money mentors, although I didn't pursue the relationship with the intention of making more money from it. I chose to flip a popular saying on its head and do things differently: I asked not what my connections could do for me but what I could do for my connections.

ASK WHAT YOU CAN DO

Every relationship comes with an exchange of value of some sort. When we choose to take on a service for someone else, we usually expect something satisfying in return. A parent gives up their time to give kids the benefit of the care and support they need. Similarly, when we work, we take up a workload so we can get paid in exchange for our time, expertise, and efforts.

The football player, actor, or entrepreneur invests hundreds or thousands of hours preparing for the big moment that benefits their game, audience, or customer. That investment can be a significant financial risk. But they take it on in the hope of reaping a big benefit. Nearly all healthy relationships come with this balance of burdens and benefits.

Your relationship with money comes with burdens and benefits too. Money can be an incredible tool, but when we take all the burdens on ourselves, then we are miserable. And when we make our relationship with money all about us and never say *thank you* to our money, then our money doesn't want to stay with us. Both situations become unsustainable losses.

However, when you take the healthy principles you've learned from your relationship with money and apply them to your relationship with other people, the impact can be incredible.

People are far more valuable than money, and yet your connections do have the potential to exponentially grow your wealth. But before you can ask what those connections will do for you, you must ask what you are willing and able to do to add more value and be of service to them.

So many people are so focused on themselves that they see connections only as a potential source of money, not as an opportunity for service. Have you ever accepted a friend request on social media only to immediately receive a message from that person trying to sell you something? How did that make you feel? Frustrated? Belittled? Used? But what if the only thing you wanted to do was ask your connections to hop on calls so you could pick their brain? Or what if you asked them for help or referrals but have never once offered to help them in some way? That isn't a good look.

That behavior signals to them that they will likely bear more burdens than reap benefits from the relationship. If you've ever found yourself in a one-sided relationship where one person gives while the other takes, you know how frustrating and exhausting it can be. Could that be why all your efforts to connect with others have ended with people simply ghosting you without an explanation as to why?

Everything we do in business is about how we communicate: with our body language, emails, texts, online videos, presentations— the list goes on. In the long term, making money is tied to the way you treat others, even though some people may seem, in the short term, to succeed without treating others well. Whether it's the relationship you have with an individual you're coaching or consulting or with your boss, team, network, or community, the way you communicate is what allows you to generate more money over time.

Don't get me wrong—when you own a business, there are times when you need to pitch your products or services or you won't get very far. But instead of looking at every individual as a dollar sign, start by making real connections with people through authentic service.

Make real connections with people through authentic service.

— Lewis Howes

BE THE BRIDGE

My dad sold life insurance for 32 years before he had the car accident that ended his career. He was an entrepreneur and launched the health insurance vertical in conjunction with Northwestern Mutual Life Insurance. My approach to enriching my connections is based on the things I witnessed him doing before social media and the Internet were a thing.

Dad was phenomenal at remembering the names of people and their family members. He wasn't pushy about trying to sell people. Instead, he genuinely connected with people on a personal level. And if they eventually came to him for insurance, then the relationship was already on a solid foundation. But he didn't lead with trying to get money from them.

Every day my dad would read the local newspaper and look for ways to encourage and celebrate community members. It didn't matter if someone was his client or not; if it made the paper and he knew the family, Dad would send relevant clippings along with a handwritten letter. Each one ended with "If I can help you with anything, let me know."

He'd always show up for people—taking meetings just to talk and looking for ways he could serve others. When I was just starting out, I did the same thing, just without the newspaper clippings. I'd reach out to people I wanted to learn from by asking if there was something I could help them with and then deliver on that need as quickly as possible without asking for anything in return. And as those different relationships grew and developed over time, I created lasting friendships built on mutual respect.

As I mentioned earlier, I went to my first mastermind group with that serving mindset. I gave and gave, expecting nothing in return. As a result, I got asked to do webinars and other promotions that generated $250,000—about half what my partner and I had made in sales the year before! I didn't go with my hand out; I offered a hand up.

Often when I asked people how I could help them, I didn't have the skill set to solve their particular challenge. Not a problem. My aim in those situations was to simply be the bridge they needed to get the help they wanted. *Who do I know who is an expert on this topic that can help?* That willingness to be the bridge got me in the door with connections as I cultivated the relationships.

I had to keep repeating my value and seeking ways to make more introductions or to add value directly with my growing skills. I did that thousands of times and not all, or even most, resulted in more money for me. But eventually opportunities began to come back to me because of my willingness to be generous. As I served my connections, more and bigger doors of opportunity opened for me. I didn't do it with that transactional mindset, but that is often how the universe works. If you put good out there, you attract good back to you.

So if you want to make more connections that could help you make more money, here is what I suggest you do. First, identify who you want to connect with. Revisit the Mapping Habit (Chapter 7) to check the destination you have in mind. Then ask these thought-starter questions:

1. Who has done at least part of what I want to do?

2. Who might have the knowledge or expertise to support me?

3. Who might be able to be the bridge and make additional connections that could be of help to me?

I suggest you generate a list of 5 to 10 names and expand as you go. Remember, this is not just about finding people from whom you can take something. Once you figure out who these people are, you'll want to first focus on providing a benefit, or many benefits, to help them get what they want. As Zig Ziglar put it, "You can have anything in life you want if you just help enough other people get what they want."[1]

I have found what I call Service Starter Questions to be powerful tools to get the conversation started:

1. What are you most excited about creating, developing, or becoming in life right now?

2. What do you see as the greatest challenge to getting there?

3. How will it make you feel when you overcome that challenge and accomplish what you want?

People will tell you a lot in how they answer those three questions. If you can help solve the challenge that is keeping them from whatever they want to create, develop, or become, you become a benefit to them. If you can do it with speed or by providing an incredible skill or service, all the better.

You don't need to get paid for it. Just think of it as helping a friend. The more you can find solutions for them, the more you appreciate in value as they appreciate your value. Worst case, if they don't appreciate your value, you have become a better person for having served others, which will likely only make you more attractive to all that is good in the world.

THE SERVICE-TO-VALUE LEVER

As the successful author, business leader, and top podcast host Patrick Bet-David shared with me, you just never know where or when these connections might bear fruit. One of those relationships began when Patrick went to a job interview in his early twenties. During the interview he decided he wasn't interested in working for the company, but he was interested in learning more from that particular interviewer and asked for the guy's card.

A few years later, Patrick reached out to the interviewer. They met for lunch every three to six months just to talk. After each conversation, Patrick asked if there was anything he could do for him. He served where he could and always sent him copies of the latest book he'd published. Years later—that's right, *years*—when Patrick had his own business, the man gave Patrick a referral. But as Patrick told me, that one referral helped him open the entire state of Florida for his business growth. According to Patrick, because he took a service approach and invested in people first, eventually money came his way.

Your value is always directly correlated to how many people you serve and how well you can serve them. Serve more? Your value goes up. That's how authentic networking works.

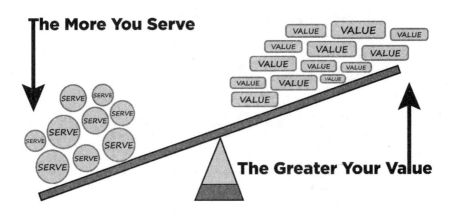

Support looks different to everyone. Maybe you can support the people in your network by showing up at their events or promoting their next project. Ask them what they need, and then just follow through on what you learn. You should also let them know how they can support you. Invite them to things you know they would enjoy and you have a connection to. Pass along recommendations you think they might find interesting. Send them a text or note of acknowledgment on random occasions without an ask attached.

If you're flaky, people just aren't going to invest in long-term relationships with you. People want to be friends with real people. The more you are yourself and the more reliable you are, the more authentic these relationships will be. The good news is that everyone can do this, including you, if you just practice the right habits and come at it with the right intention.

The people you really want to work with are people who really want to work with you.

— Lewis Howes

Remember, this all takes time. Quality relationships don't happen overnight, but showing up consistently for people over the long haul speaks volumes. If you want to stand out in your relationships, show up, be true to your word, be a good person, and always think of how you can add value.

More likely than not, you're like me and want authentic relationships. The good news is that most people are the same way. Be yourself. Give others the gift of the real you so they know they can be themselves too.

It'll take the relationships to the next level when neither of you is putting on a show—and it will be way less effort. The people you really want to work with are people who really want to work with you.

FIND YOUR FINANCIAL MENTORS

Authenticity and vulnerability are the keys to creating lasting relationships with the people whose authority and level of success feel aspirational to you. Surround yourself with people and mentors who can help you start conversations about money. Pick up on their mindset, how they approach investing and wealth building, and more.

I'm constantly talking with people who have achieved massive financial success so I can learn from them and reflect on what I can do to change and improve my life. This is why I love being a part of mastermind groups.

Masterminds are collective groups of growth-minded individuals with some common ground. People come into them wanting to network and help others by collaborating and sharing a knowledge base or skill set. They can also help get your message in front of their audiences.

If you are currently struggling to make ends meet or are trying to heal your relationship with money after going into debt, I wouldn't recommend that you go more deeply into debt to join a mastermind group. It may be more beneficial to investigate some local mentoring programs or business networking groups at Rotary

Clubs, your local chamber of commerce, or business networking groups.

But with that being said, most mastermind groups do not require you to go into debt. There are different kinds of masterminds based on income levels. Or you could start a simple money mastermind group of your own with a book club that meets once a month to discuss a money book of your choice. You could start with *Make Money Easy* as a guide and follow the exercises at the end of chapters together to support one another as you heal your money wounds and break through your money mindset barriers.

As part of the two-way street, the people in the group want you to bring your best so that they can give their best to you. This means that every group offers the opportunity for you to grow your best and receive the best of others. That's where I started—a free mastermind book club that was reading *Think and Grow Rich*. It was just a way for people to build a network and talk about the concepts in the book.

Once you've worked together through the first book, you'll have a well-established group of people who are open to having conversations about money. You will have accountability as you continue to learn more. You'll have a group that will push you out of your comfort zone while helping you become more financially literate. Within six months to a year, you'll have so much more knowledge and confidence that you will be pushed into your next mastermind, or you could continue to expand your group by networking with people in your local area or bringing in a guest speaker.

Anytime I invest in going to a mastermind with people who are at a different level than I am, I take away at least one new idea or make one connection that ends up being more valuable than the money I put into it. It's all about being around people who are doing the things you want to do and embracing the chance to learn about what others have overcome. When you discover what they've done to speed up their timelines, you begin to see new possibilities for yourself and your business.

When you are at a point when you can invest in higher-level masterminds, I believe something unlocks inside you, or at least it did for me. I felt inspired. I was very present and focused. I'm not saying that being around people who are wealthier than you means you'll automatically make more money. But being there should support your own ability to make money.

Once you do the research and find the mastermind group that feels right for you, it's time to act. Find ways to add value to the group. Create connection points by showing up. Masterminds can create a certain level of urgency to make it work because you have skin in the game. You can remind yourself that you want to get a return on your investment, and it will help you see the value in actively participating.

It's normal to feel uncomfortable when you join a group and find yourself in a room with new people. That's what growth is all about. If you get to the point where you're sharing information and you feel like you're the smartest person in the room, it may be time to invite some new people into the conversation whose success is a level or two above yours. It'll stretch you and humble you at the same time.

Once you get intentional about engaging your network in an authentic way, it's time to add the next habit and learn how to lead others to enroll in your vision.

YOUR GAME PLAN

Exercise 1: Offer to Help

If you want to tip the balance of the value scale, you must begin to serve others. That starts by identifying who you know and offering to help. Start by making a list of 10 people you know who could use the kind of help you can provide. In a second column, write what you know about their goals and obstacles. Finally, in a third column, write a concrete, practical way you could help or add value to each of them.

Use these questions to spark your thinking about ways to serve:

- Who do I know whom they should know?

- What can I do to connect these two people in a way that benefits them both?

- What is a need I see them having that I can provide an answer to?
- What is their Meaningful Mission?
- How can I support them to further their Meaningful Mission?

Name	Goals/Obstacles	How I Can Help
Britt Anderson	Wants to serve nonprofits with her coaching service/ needs to broaden her connections	I can connect her with my friend Dale who hosts a podcast for nonprofit leaders.

Now comes the fun part. Take a moment to text, email, or call each person on the list and simply offer to help. It may take a moment for them to understand the offer, but tell them you are trying to work on your generosity muscles. Listen to what they say and then deliver. If they seem interested, offer to do the specific step you wrote in the third column while asking nothing in return.

Doing this will help unlock something in you and tell the universe you are a good steward of what you have and you're ready to receive more.

Exercise 2: Start a Money Mastermind

You don't have to spend a lot of money to start your own mastermind. In fact, you can do it for free. Google a list of five books about money that interest you, and for each book write its name and one thing that interests you about it.

1. **Example:** *Money: Master the Game* by Tony Robbins. I'm interested in this book because my friends Thomas and Finola recommended it and they are some of the most financially successful people I know.

2. _____

3. _____

4. _____

5. _____

6. _____

Now think of four to six people you could invite to read these books with you and get together in person or virtually on video to discuss.

1. _____

2. _____

3. _____

4. _____

5. _____

6. _____

Reach out and invite them to join your money mastermind. What gets scheduled gets done, so put your meetings on the calendar so you stay accountable. When you get together, talk about the lessons you learned from the book and pay attention to what stands out for the others. As you deepen your trust, have authentic and vulnerable conversations and look for ways to serve each other well.

CHAPTER TEN

HABIT 5: THE MAGNETIC HABIT

Become an Enrollment Artist

Almost everything good in my life came because I deployed the Magnetic Habit. That's quite a claim, I know, but it's true. Habit 5 is all about the power of enrollment—the art of inviting others to get on board with whatever you are doing. All the opportunities I've enjoyed, not only to make money but also in sports, business, and relationships, came my way because I learned how to enroll and lead others to believe in and follow my vision in some way.

Back when my biggest dream was to compete in professional sports, I knew a good first step was to become an all-American athlete. I needed to enroll a coach to guide me if I hoped to make it. I enrolled the coach I really wanted for support in track-and-field events by casting my vision to her. Then I took the leap and made the commitment: "I'll do whatever you tell me."

That got her attention. "Okay," she told me, "there's a chance you can be an all-American, but you have to do *everything* I tell you for the next six months."

I kept my word. I dedicated all my time and energy to that goal. I sacrificed a lot of time with friends and missed several fun events, but my coach knew I was serious and willing to learn with her instead of making it my way or the highway. As a result, I became a two-time all-American athlete in football and track-and-field.

In my senior year of college, I went to the Ohio State scouting combine with a backpack full of highlight reel DVDs. I handed them to each NFL scout at the event and introduced myself: "Hi, I'm Lewis. This is what I can do. Can I have your business card?" I followed up with every one of them, enrolling them in who I was and what I could deliver on the field.

I ended up with a tryout for both the Cleveland Browns and the Buffalo Bills. I didn't make either team, but someone I met at that combine gave my highlight video to a coach and that set me up for the opportunity to play professional football in the Arena League.

That's the power of enrollment: being willing to put yourself out there and convey to other people that you are ready for the possibility of greater opportunities. Putting in the hard work and long hours, along with achieving consistently high-level results, spoke volumes to those watching me. When I embraced their constructive criticism so I could get better, it showed them I wasn't messing around. I chose to be fully present with my coaches, recruiters, other players, and my team.

My passion and commitment answered the unspoken questions about whether I was worth their time, resources, and relational equity. You see, enrollment is more than just charisma or salesmanship. It's how to show up to demonstrate that you are confident about your goals and to invite them to join you in that vision. The more excited you are about what you're doing, the more people will be excited to work with you.

POWERED BY PASSION

Enrollment begins with passion and expands to fill the size of your mission. Entrepreneur, coach, and best-selling author of *The Power of One More,* Ed Mylett is one of the best enrollers I've ever met. When I asked him how he learned the art of enrollment, Ed told me he once read a book called *Selling the Dream* by Guy Kawasaki:

The book's premise was that great leaders are evangelical about their cause. They sell a big enough dream so that the dreams of all the people within their stewardship can fit inside the one they're selling. Great evangelists learn to link their cause and their mission to someone else's bliss.[1]

When I met Internet pioneer, *New York Times* best-selling author, keynote speaker, and social media strategist Joel Comm, I was a nobody with only two minutes to talk to him at a conference that we were both attending. But I enrolled him when I explained why I believed LinkedIn would soon be a powerful social media platform to use in business.

Frankly, I didn't think I had made a huge impact in that two-minute conversation. In my mind I was just some young, unknown guy who had the opportunity to talk to a highly motivated and successful person. A few months later, however, he emailed me with an opportunity to join him as a speaker at an online social media workshop. He told me that because I had talked so passionately about LinkedIn, unlike anyone he had seen speak on the topic before, he wanted me to join him in the workshop. My enthusiasm for what excited me excited him.

Back then in 2009, I had no experience with webinars. None at all. But I still jumped in with both feet. I did the best I could to add value during my presentation, and in just one hour, I made $6,200 by offering a course at the end of my talk. I was blown away. That experience unlocked a world of moneymaking opportunities that I had no clue even existed before that day. Just a passionate, two-minute conversation converted into a massive opportunity that changed the trajectory of my entire growth path.

Despite that two-minute conversation success, I learned that enrollment is not a one-and-done event. It can take time to produce fruit, so you have to be patient. You must consistently show up and follow up, and always be ready to give it your all.

Enrollment is not a one-and-done event.

— Lewis Howes

When I first read *The 4-Hour Workweek* by Tim Ferriss, I had thought that someday I wanted to write a best-selling book like Tim's. However, since I nearly flunked out of English class my senior year of high school, I knew I needed extra help in publishing a book. As I read the acknowledgments in Tim's book, I saw that he thanked his agent, Stephen Hanselman. *That's who I want to be my agent*, I thought.

Now, I was a nobody at that time. I had no audience. I had never met Stephen. But I decided I would seek opportunities to enroll him in becoming my agent *over time*. I started by following him on Facebook and leaving him messages occasionally to let him know I was interested in partnering someday. He was polite to me and agreed I wasn't yet ready to launch a best-selling book.

A year later I saw that Tim Ferriss was hosting an event with some of the biggest leaders he could find, including multiple *New York Times* bestsellers and folks from the publishing world. As I looked at the agenda of topics for the event, I saw how I could add unique value to the event by leveraging my growing LinkedIn expertise to talk about virtual book tours. I had recently done a webinar and sold more than 800 books in that one webinar alone. I knew webinars could play a significant role in promoting books for all authors, but it hadn't really been done before.

I crafted a passionate email to Tim's assistant, with whom I had already built a connection, explaining how I could bring value to the event. I knew I couldn't bring name recognition or sell event seats, so I offered to do it for free. He loved the idea and forwarded my email to Tim. Before I knew it, I was on a call with Tim Ferriss—he, too, loved the idea and wanted me to speak!

At that point I would not have considered myself a writer. I had written a small book about LinkedIn that I co-wrote with another mentor, but that was it. Still, there I was on stage at the event with Tim Ferriss himself interviewing me about virtual book tours. All because I had patiently and passionately enrolled people into my vision.

Midway through the event, Tim introduced me backstage to his literary agent, the same one I wanted to work with someday,

Stephen Hanselman. This was my chance. A lot of people would have jumped at that moment and tried to pitch him on the spot, thinking it was now or never. But I knew I still wasn't ready yet to work with him.

I told Stephen, "Hey, now's not the right time, but I would love to do a book with you in the future. Can we stay in touch and keep that conversation going?" He happily agreed. Over time I offered ways to serve him and bring value without expecting anything in return. Every six months or so, I messaged him and asked how I could support him or which authors I could help promote as I built my own brand and audience.

Four years later, after I had launched *The School of Greatness* show and kept putting more and more content out into the world, Stephen reached out to me. "I think it's time we did a book together." And that was that! It took over five years to manifest, but my vision of writing a *New York Times* bestseller had become a reality because I was willing to do the work to add value, continue to develop my skills and service, and enroll people over time.

THE PATH TO GREATNESS

I'm so grateful that *The School of Greatness* show has become known for the high-caliber guests I interview to learn from their expertise. But it hasn't always been easy to enroll those guests to appear on the show.

For example, it took four years to enroll Tony Robbins to be on the show. As a speaker, leader, and author of many best-selling books such as *Unlimited Power* and *Awaken the Giant Within*, he always has a full plate. At one point I told his team that I would be willing to hop on a plane anytime to meet with him anywhere. They took my offer literally.

Tony's team offered me a 45-minute window with Tony in Los Angeles—while he was in his plane on the runway. I jumped at the chance, rearranged my schedule, and began to think that I would love to capture this interview on video. Up to that time, my show was only audio, so I enrolled a video team to join me when I sat down with Tony on that runway.

That episode exploded with well over a million views of the video, and *The School of Greatness* show forged new ground into the video format that has become its signature style. Since then my relationship with Tony has grown, and he has been on the show repeatedly. To this day, I am sure my flexibility and passion to meet with him showed that I was willing to take the time to invest and truly bring value to him. We formed the foundation for a mutually beneficial relationship once I demonstrated that my vision aligned with his vision.

The same thing is true when I seek to enroll speakers for my annual Summit of Greatness event. I've always sought to deliver the highest value for the audience, so bringing in people who can deliver that value has always been key. Previous speakers have included Esther Perel, Jen Sincero, Jay Shetty, Gabby Bernstein, Maria Sharapova, Brendon Burchard, Eric Thomas, Jesse Itzler, Dr. Caroline Leaf, Erwin McManus, David Goggins, Dr. Joe Dispenza, and many others.

Those people don't come because I pay them a lot of money; in fact, we rarely pay them anything. They don't come simply because I send an email inviting them and sharing the value we can offer them at our event. They come because my team and I invest time to actively enroll them in the vision of the event and by offering a lot of value over time. Often the invite is simply the next step in the natural progression of our relationship. Each of them has already been a guest on the show, so it is simply about taking the next step.

However, we do put a lot of intentional effort into making the experience an incredible one for them. First, I ask how I can promote them or their books, help with their connections, and find ways to showcase the message they want to share.

I also let them know that we do give them a memorable experience: first-class flights, top hotel rooms, media content for them to reach millions of people—whatever would make the event special for them. We greet them at the airport and chauffeur them right to their hotel. When they arrive in their hotel room, they find pictures of their families already framed and welcoming them as if they have come home. They discover their favorite foods are already waiting for them. We provide a full photo shoot for them with a top-notch photographer.

In short, I show how much I value their time and the special people they are. Because of that, they tell their friends. "Hey, I may not have made a lot, but that Lewis guy really gave me an incredible experience. If you ever get a chance to speak at that event, take it!"

On the other hand, I've interacted with plenty of people who do not practice this Magnetic Habit and have not learned how to enroll. These are the people who send a cold email and say, "Can I be on your show? It would really help me out. Look how cool I am!" They don't offer anything; it's just about them. So usually I leave the conversation with these people in the same place. Because if people aren't willing to listen and find out how they can help me, I'm not going to expect myself to do more for them.

The way you do your outreach sets the expectation for how you'll treat others. If you start the conversation with the focus on yourself, you aren't inviting someone to grow with you. You're inviting them to reward you for emailing them. But if your actions create a sincere culture of mutual growth, people will be much more likely to want to buy what you are selling.

ENROLLMENT IN EVERY MOMENT

Every step of my journey to make money has taught me this reality: enrollment isn't a one-time thing; it happens at every moment. Every day, you're either enrolling others or being enrolled in someone else's vision. And you are either enrolling or unenrolling people in you and your vision.

Your attitude, energy, and presence in every moment and situation determine your enrollment success. You're either enrolling someone in liking you, trusting you, and respecting you more, or you're unenrolling them based on your negative actions, words, or way of being. I'm not saying you have to be perfect all the time, but you'll have more success enrolling others when you intentionally and consistently present who you are every day in every way. Your way of being shows the results you consistently create.

The way
you do your
outreach sets
the expectation
for how you'll
treat others.

— Lewis Howes

If I'm looking to get in shape and someone says they're a personal trainer but they're 100 pounds overweight, I'm not enrolled in them. If they can't do it for themselves, why would I hire them to do it for me? Or if you're a jerk to someone upon first meeting them, you'll likely unenroll them from anything you care about because of how you acted.

But what happens when people do *not* cultivate this Magnetic Habit? In short, nothing they want in life tends to come their way, including money and everything else that makes life richer. When someone doesn't enroll well, every dream, goal, or accomplishment becomes exponentially more difficult to achieve because what they need is simply unavailable to them. If they want a job, to work with someone, to marry someone—you name it—everything gets so much tougher.

As a result they end up feeling isolated, suffering, stressed, and drained, all because they can't enroll anyone to join them. If you are an unenrolling person, no one wants to hang out with you, be your colleague, hire you, or give you opportunities to make more money. Think about it: Would you want to help someone who has a selfish attitude, doesn't take care of themselves, is never on time, and treats people poorly? Probably not.

Unless that person has some unique and incredible talent, no one will want to work with them for long. And even then, they will likely eventually lose their credibility or reputation and even the money that may have initially come to them as a result of their talents.

One important thing to know is that not everyone will be enrolled in you or your vision all the time, and that's okay. In fact, it's a good thing. The last thing you want to do is try to force people to take a journey with you when they really are not aligned with the direction you are going. That sets the stage for toxic relationships in your life that can drag you down, not lift you up.

Another reality is that some people will be enrolled in you for only a season of life. We've had team members who were critical pieces of our growth for a season who then chose to move on because their life priorities had shifted and they needed to make a change. That's also part of the journey. It is rare that the same people who you begin the journey with are still with you as you grow unless they grow within your vision as well.

At times I have beaten myself up when that happens, thinking that they might not have left if I were a more effective leader. Yes, I always need to improve and grow in my leadership skills, but not everyone is the right fit at that season of time. And that's okay. It's better to let those people go than to try to make it work and be left with frustration all around.

WHAT LIES BENEATH?

If you aren't expecting to enroll people, you might miss important opportunities. For example, Grant Cardone told me about his interesting experience on the television show *Undercover Billionaire*. Grant wanted to expose the myth that it takes money to make money. He firmly believes that making money is all about creating the right contacts with people and that those *contacts* can become *contracts* that generate equity over time. But his vision all centers on one thing—you need to enroll people to invest.

On the show, he was dropped off in a town where he didn't know anyone, and he couldn't use any money to make a business deal. He essentially had to make something happen from nothing. After rolling up in an old pickup truck, Grant walked into his first undercover meeting sporting a new look—a shaved head. He started a conversation with someone at the meeting who was looking for investor money but assumed Grant was just a nobody. The entire conversation was consumed with this guy bragging about how much money he had and talking down to undercover Grant.

This guy didn't realize that the person he treated like a nobody was probably the biggest potential investor he had ever met. The longer the conversation went, the more he made himself the center of it. And the less he invited Grant to be included, the less Grant was interested in listening—or investing. As a result the man missed a massive investment opportunity for his company's future.

Grant told me that he learned two massive lessons in that exchange. "One, you don't know who you're dealing with. More importantly, you don't know who they're going to become."[2] Maybe the person who just followed you on social media doesn't have anything impressive on their résumé now, but over time, that person may surprise you. Even if a person seems to be "nothing" now, they could have a huge company or successful brand in 10 years. If you develop a positive relationship now, they may want to support you later.

Think of it like this: Imagine you own a mining company. You want to get rich by turning that company into a profit producer. Then you meet two people. One owns hundreds of acres of land. It sounds impressive! The other owns only 10 acres. Not so impressive. With which one should you most want to connect?

The best answer is *both*. You simply have no idea what value is hidden beneath the surface of either property. Maybe the hundreds of acres are worthless and the 10 acres are filled with gold. On the other hand, the hundreds of acres might have gold—and the 10 acres are full of diamonds. You just never know based on what you see on the surface. You've got to be willing to dig into the relationship to discover what it has to offer.

When you engage others with an enrolling mindset, you set your relationship default to invite rather than invest. You don't start by asking people to put money into your company. You start by engaging in authentic conversations. On the other hand, when you disengage people by unenrolling them (lying, appearing disconnected, not holding to your word, etc.) you block them out of your future. You're closing the door not just on them but also on yourself because you lose any opportunity for them to grow with you.

Every moment of every day, you have the choice to enroll or unenroll. Making enrolling a habit sets you on the path that is most likely to attract more money to you, while unenrollment consistently spirals into failure. It's your choice.

It's about wanting to be a blessing instead of being a burden.

— Lewis Howes

In my experience very few people who genuinely live out their Meaningful Mission can do so without naturally enrolling others into that vision. Don't get me wrong: There are people out there who have a lot of money and no intention of serving others. But I have found that a deeper feeling of peace and fulfillment comes as a result of enrolling others through service to them. It's not about having a hero complex that demands you rescue people; it's just about wanting to be a blessing instead of being a burden.

When you passionately share your vision with others and invite them to come along, you give people the opportunity to enroll with you. They may simply subscribe and follow or find deeper ways to support your mission because they've been drawn to who you are and your mission. The truth is that the real investment they are making is in you.

MAGNETIZE YOUR BRAND

Your brand is all about who you are. And who you are determines your ability to enroll others to follow you. That's why if you want to attract money, you must learn to lead people, and ultimately, learn to lead yourself. Leadership guru John C. Maxwell says that if you think you are a leader but have no followers, you're not leading. You're merely taking a walk.[3] The same principle applies to enrollment. If people are not following you and your brand, you haven't gotten good at enrollment.

Super Bowl champion Steve Weatherford told me there are certain men he will follow just based on seeing them for the first time when they walk in a room because he senses something about their presence that he respects. As a former pro athlete, he assesses "how broad their shoulders are" as a way of measuring how disciplined they are with nutrition and fitness. If they lead themselves well in that area, he thinks they are likely to lead themselves well in other areas. I think the same can be said for everyone in many ways.

I call it the **Personal Power Principle:** *How well you lead yourself determines your personal power to lead others.* The better you lead yourself, the more potential you have to enroll others, move your mission forward, and possibly improve your financial situation.

And how do you build your personal power? There's an easy way to do it every single day. David Goggins is a retired Navy SEAL and the only member of the U.S. Armed Forces to complete SEAL training, U.S. Army Ranger School, and Air Force tactical air controller training. I asked him how he leads himself well in the face of whatever adversity comes his way.

David told me the key was leading himself well in the little things to start every day. Before he ever opens his phone first thing in the morning, he does at least 15 little things that give him a series of wins to lead him to a positive place. It could be something like shaving his head, working out, or even cleaning the bathroom. All of it gives him powerful momentum.

I think of this daily practice as *win stacking*—starting every day with a series of intentional wins. I like adding gratitudes into this mix as well, to express what I am most thankful for. By stacking wins and gratitudes together, I multiply their impact and prepare myself mentally to lead myself well and generate more personal power that will naturally enroll others to follow.

With this leadership focus in mind, here are three critical groups of people you will need to enroll on a regular basis to make money easier and enjoy a richer life:

1. **Yourself.** Learning how to improve your ability to enroll others doesn't start with putting on a crown and expecting people to follow you. It begins with you being intentional and taking the time to enroll your first follower—yourself.

   Ask yourself: *What does someone I want to follow look like?* They probably model integrity, responsibility, and accountability. Maybe there are other principles you admire that magnetize you. Commit to showing up like that healthy human being. Strengthen your emotional awareness by learning how to navigate your own emotions. If you need a coach or therapist, start there. I have found that professional help can be a great mirror to spot the places in yourself that are filled with potential to grow but that sometimes are just hiding in your blind spots.

Work on sharpening your communication skills. Ask people questions. Be thoughtful and polite. Spend time getting clarity on your vision and how to involve others so you can create fulfillment and peace at every financial level of your life. Enrolling yourself is a daily process to become confident that you will first follow yourself. Once you feel confident in that, you can move to the next area.

2. **Others**. Self-enrollment gives you the ability to set an example of authenticity and vulnerability. Sharing your passion for personal growth can inspire others to invest in their own journeys of growth. Celebrate their successes and offer support as they face challenges. Make it known that you're available to them when they feel low or to share the load when they have taken on too much. Be present. Create a sense of mutual growth and authentic connection.

   When you enroll others in the pursuit of personal excellence by serving them, you not only help them level up their potential but also create a network of growth-minded people willing to help each other thrive. Those people who look to you for that guidance will be the ones who consistently return to work with you over time.

3. **Your team**. Some of the people on your team will become brand ambassadors. They'll stand out from the crowd and be true advocates for your vision. These are the people Ed Mylett calls "evangelizers." I would call them your magnetic team.

   These are the ones who plan on going through whatever adversity your business, organization, or unit goes through. You can empower your team members by helping them align their personal goals with the collective vision. Share the dream and inspire them to see themselves as an important part of it. Encourage them to share their wins and concerns honestly and openly. Give them opportunities to collaborate by using their strengths to support a workplace where creativity flows freely.

If you create a culture that is supportive of professional development and continuous improvement, then your team will begin enrolling others and exponentially multiplying your network. By enrolling your team and hiring the people who buy into your vision, you create an environment that is capable of overcoming challenges with grace and achieving extraordinary results.

It has been said that the first job of every leader is to define reality for the people they lead. That aligns with what legendary inspirational thinker and author Wayne Dyer said: "Our intentions create our reality."[4] All too often people don't fully understand their own intentions. That ignorance undermines their mission because how they present their mission will determine how others perceive it.

Great enrollers create win-win conversations by asking, "How can I help?" and inviting the other person to respond in kind. But if you don't follow through, it would have been better for you to never have asked because people can see through insincerity. When you genuinely want people to be a part of your purpose, then you can expand your dream and bring others with you. If your mission is an exclusive club that only serves you, you should expect to walk alone.

Let's say you want a raise at your job. That's not a bad goal as long as you don't make it all about making more money just because you think you deserve it or you want it. Instead, look for a win-win by asking yourself, *How can I be of greater service to truly meet a need for the company?*

If you're trying to sell a product or service and need to find potential customers to enroll, ask yourself, *Who would benefit most from my help? Who is experiencing pain or has a problem that I can solve with this product or service?* Then package your value to help someone remove the pain or to get results faster, better, or cheaper.

It may also help to view enrollment as a game. Playful energy is magnetic. When you approach enrollment with that playful energy, it doesn't feel as overwhelming, stressful, or daunting if you get rejected. When you get a no, simply reflect on your approach and consider any failures as feedback to improve and grow. Maybe the timing is just off for that person or you didn't communicate effectively. Perhaps it's just that you need to learn more skills or improve your offer.

Whatever the reason for a no, don't take it personally and never give your power away. Slow down enough to stay open to understanding and discerning the context of the situation. Instead of stopping and giving up completely, ask yourself how you can improve for the next time. And find a way to make it fun!

One of the best lessons you can learn is how to become improvisational in your communication by asking questions like the following:

- Is there anything else I could do to help support you and your team?

- Is there something else I could possibly interest you in?

- If things change later, will you please let me know?

Even when the situation doesn't look like it will work in your favor in the moment, by being willing to pivot in the moment, you become more magnetic. As you continue to patiently pursue your mission, you never know when the situation might change down the road.

YOUR GAME PLAN

Take a moment to consider the type of leader you are right now compared to the enrolling leader you know you could be.

- How do you currently define your role as a leader?
- How enrolling or unenrolling are you?
- What are the values that guide your leadership style?
- How do you handle challenges and setbacks?
- Which areas of your leadership could benefit from further training?

- How do you enroll and empower those around you to reach their full potential?
- What strategies do you use to build trust and foster positive relationships with your team?

Exercise 1: Create Your Enrolling Blueprint

If the concept of enrolling others is new to you, then it's a good idea to take the time to get clear on what exactly you are enrolling people to do. To do this, work through these questions.

- What's your Meaningful Mission? (If you aren't sure, check out *The Greatness Mindset* book.)
- What's your vision for this Meaningful Mission?
- Why is it important?
- Who will it help?
- How will it make a difference in the world?
- How could the people you hope to enroll come along with you on the journey?
- How will it benefit them personally?
- Why did you choose this particular person to enroll?

When you understand the answers to these questions, they serve as the backbone of your "elevator pitch" that helps you articulate your vision and draw people to you.

Exercise 2: Look in the Mirror

While what you say is important and does help enroll others, it's what they *see* that makes you stand out. And when what they see demonstrates confidence, wisdom, and strong self-leadership, that makes you a magnet and attracts the kind of people you want to surround you. This exercise is simple: when you think about who you are, beyond just physical appearance, how would you describe yourself?

If your description includes things that are positive and likely to pull people to you, call them out and celebrate them. These should be acknowledged and deepened.

If your description includes things that are more negative or holding you back, be honest with yourself. Will you commit to doing something about it? If so, start today to make strides to lead yourself better.

The purpose of this exercise is not to make you feel bad about yourself; rather, it's to celebrate what is working and look for ways to improve.

Remember, you are enough, and you are becoming more.

Exercise 3: Win Stacking

Little wins early in the day can lead to sustained momentum. If you aren't starting your day with intentionality, it can quickly get away from you. To help start your day positively, brainstorm a list of three to five little things you can do that will set you up for success.

Write them on a notecard or on a note in your phone and make a habit of checking them off each day to build a habit of win stacking. Use this momentum of small wins to drive you forward as you pursue big goals. As this momentum builds, it will cause a change in you that will be evident to those around you—making you more magnetic in the process.

CHAPTER ELEVEN

HABIT 6: THE MOBILITY HABIT

Delegate to Empower Others

My first marketing company ended in disaster. When my business partner and I initially started working together, we figured if we each were good at different skills, then the two of us together would be great. We thought that together we would simply scale and create more value for more people—and earn more money too. We couldn't have been more wrong.

Problems emerged almost immediately as we grew because neither of us knew how to hire or train effective team members. We brought on a few fantastic freelancers, but I still held the mindset that if I wanted to be successful, I had to do most of the work on my own.

I pushed myself day in and day out. I assumed we both would go all out, focusing on what we each were good at while naturally covering each other's blind spots. The problem was we were assuming the same things. When I kept working without taking a rest, it eventually left me burned out and resentful toward my partner.

Unfortunately, instead of working together to grow our knowledge and skills, we fought, which only pushed us further apart. We both lost our direction, and neither of us had any idea how to make it stop. What made it worse was that our focus on profits made us push harder because we feared losing marketplace momentum.

Even though we grew our revenue every quarter, we couldn't keep up with the increasingly crushing workload. We made more money but felt paralyzed. We had dreamed that our business would be like a pyramid, with the team expanding as we grew. We assumed that the more the pyramid grew, the lighter our load would be. But it felt like every advance we made only led us deeper into a new circle of hell.

What we thought was momentum was just the weight of our success. Turns out that our pyramid was upside down because everyone depended on us. Don't get me wrong: everyone on that team was smart and hardworking. But in a way, that only made our failure more frustrating. My partner and I could only create so much by working more. In fact, by working harder instead of learning how to delegate and mobilize more people effectively, we slowed our ability to make money easy.

THE HELICOPTER ENTREPRENEUR

At some point on your money journey, you may want to start a side hustle or business. If you're like me, you might not set out to start a business but instead accidentally fall into becoming an entrepreneur just by doing what you love to do. It may only remain a side hustle for you, but if you are good at what you do, it is likely to grow.

When you launch a business, it is not uncommon to think you must do everything yourself. Yes, you may be good at one thing, but that one thing can only take you so far. If all you do is push yourself to do more, be more, and produce more, you will probably burn out. And your business, however large it may have become, will probably suffer.

In my experience, we entrepreneurs have an almost parental instinct that causes us to think that the business is totally dependent on us. After all, your company is like your baby. In a moment of passion, you made this amazing organization. You nurtured it, held it, and celebrated every little milestone. Now someone is telling you that you're supposed to trust someone else to handle it while you just . . . what? Sleep?

Actually, yes, that's exactly what you need to do because, like any healthy child, a healthy business needs to grow. And for that to happen, eventually you need to get out of the way.

When I started trying to expand that first business, I had no idea how to hire or manage people. I thought everyone would just work the same way I did. I was wrong. I had to learn how to become a better leader. I had to learn how to delegate and build processes. It took time to realize that what I was great at was only one piece of the puzzle. I had to learn how to let go of my baby. I did not do a good job of that at first. But I learned from my mistakes and from the many experts I've had the privilege of talking with over the years.

Trusting other people with your business baby can bring a lot of different emotions to the surface, but you only have three choices: delegate and grow, stay where you are, or fail. I assume you don't want your business to fail and you'd prefer it grow and make more money for you, so . . . *delegate* it is.

Let's talk about how this works in real life.

In any business there are a lot of different things to manage—team, payroll, accounting, marketing, product development, customer service, taxes, human resources, logistics, and tons more. You're probably a rock star in some of these areas. But admit it: You are at best average at the rest, and you might be downright bad at some of them. And that's okay. The one thing you do need to get good at is leadership. As leadership guru John C. Maxwell says, "Everything rises and falls on leadership." What John calls Level 2 leadership is where most solopreneurs struggle: people. Delegating isn't about just telling people about your positional authority or title; it's about developing emotional intelligence and learning a new set of people skills to lead well.

You need others to do truly great things.

— Lewis Howes

At first you may need to do everything yourself as you get started. But at some point, you need to give your business the room to take its first steps. You can be ready to steady it if it starts to stumble, but being a helicopter entrepreneur will only wear you out. Hovering will only keep your business crawling instead of walking and eventually running, which is what you need it to do to potentially make more money for you.

That is why you need the Mobility Habit. If you want to scale what you do and move further and faster for greater impact, you need to learn to delegate ruthlessly.

IF YOU WANT SOMETHING DONE . . .

Napoleon Bonaparte is often credited with saying if you want something done right, do it yourself. To that I say, if you want something done great, do it with others. If I remember my history, Napoleon's advice didn't work out so well for him, and it won't work well for you either. You need others to do truly great things.

Delegation is the art of giving responsibility to people you've enrolled to support you. Giving them that responsibility equips them with the ability to contribute to your Meaningful Mission. Sure, there is some risk in delegating, but that risk opens the door for exponential rewards you otherwise could not get.

Plus, when you delegate, you get to leverage your strengths and focus on the parts of your job you love. In his best-selling book *Mind Shift*, my friend Erwin McManus says that we should be average in just about everything. Rather than trying to be great at everything, Erwin suggests we should focus on those areas where we can be truly spectacular and leave everything else to other people. When we do that, we unleash the potential for greatness in ourselves and everyone else.

You need
to give your
business the
room to take
its first steps.

— Lewis Howes

Delegation empowers your team, but it can be hard to hand over control to someone else. If you aren't intentional about it, you'll find yourself looking over people's shoulders and getting frustrated when they can't read your mind, and finally end up just doing it yourself. But when people don't feel empowered, you make your fears about their failure come to life. Instead of being freed to deliver their best, they focus on not upsetting the boss: you. As a result, they get distracted, which simply affirms your belief that only you can do it. Meanwhile, the reality is that it was your lack of delegation that caused it.

I know because I've done it too. I wanted everything to be done right, so I did it myself. I got even less work done because I ended up redoing the work I quasi-delegated. I spent the rest of my time looking over my team's shoulders.

Fear undermines vision and is the enemy of delegation. But when you delegate confidently, your team can become upwardly mobile. You free everyone to give it their best. Your team learns to be flexible and keep moving forward in the face of challenges. You begin to realize that you don't have to double-check everything as they prove themselves to be capable.

The best part is that the Mobility Habit really accelerates when you start enrolling other people to help.

KNOW YOUR WORTH

I suggest you start delegating by considering three ways to create leverage that I learned from entrepreneur and investor Naval Ravikant: code, media, and labor.

Code refers to creating software that can be used by other people to make more money for you and add value to them. It also applies to delegating because you can use software or code other people have written to delegate effectively. What you used to have to pay someone else to do can now often be done via an app or technology of some sort. Start to delegate tasks for both you and your team by looking for ways to leverage code and technology.

For example, a friend of mine whose team does a lot of writing used to have someone manually create transcripts of meetings. Now they have found ways to leverage AI technology to automate that process and save both time and money while preserving quality. Your industry will be different, but I guarantee there are already numerous ways you can find to put technology to work to save yourself time, which *is* money.

Media has to do with leveraging video, audio, and other content creation options to spread your message or reach. You can only be in so many places at once, but media can be replicated to multiply your impact.

This strategy is at the heart of what we do all day, every day, at Greatness Media. Once we record an episode for *The School of Greatness* show, for example, we then get creative to put that media to use in a variety of ways and across multiple social platforms. In this way we use both media and technology to create leverage and essentially delegate our outreach to these tools and platforms.

Media allows you to become more mobile. It frees your message to go further faster than you could ever have done on your own. Even this book is a tool I am leveraging to reach you right now. I can't be with everyone all the time to share insights and help them grow, but this book can get tucked in a bag, taken on an airplane, or listened to while you work out. Because I chose to delegate in this way, the media with my message makes its way to you.

The third way to create leverage is labor, or delegating to people. For most people, especially as they are just getting started, this is the area they will focus on as the best next step. That being said, most people struggle to let go and hand off responsibilities to others.

But think about this: How much is your time worth? Have you ever done the math to find out? Simply divide the amount of money you expect to make over the course of a year by the number of hours you plan to put into it, and you have your basic hourly rate.

For example, to keep the numbers easy, let's presume you expect to make $50,000 a year after investing 1,920 hours (40 per week for 48 weeks): $50,000 / 1,920 = $26.04 per hour. It may help to see how this formula would apply across several different annual amounts (rounded for clarity):

Annual Amount	Number of Hours	Hourly Rate (Rounded)
$50,000	1,920	$26
$100,000	1,920	$52
$150,000	1,920	$78
$200,000	1,920	$104
$250,000	1,920	$130

If you presently expect to make $100,000 each year, your hourly rate is approximately $52. That's what your time is worth to you right now. So it only makes sense that if there are things you are doing right now that you could pay someone less than $52 an hour to do for you, you probably should do it. With your newly added free time, you can devote more energy to increasing your annual amount either through your business, a side hustle, or expanding your career options.

Now, notice something especially powerful here. As your annual amount increases, your own hourly rate goes up as well. Which means there are more and more tasks that you should be willing to pay someone else to do for you. What are the key things that produce your annual amount? How can you delegate so you can do more of those things and make more money? In fact, I suggest that the fastest way to increase your annual amount is to delegate these tasks to other people.

To help figure out what tasks you may want to delegate, ask these three questions:

1. **What *do* I do?** Do a brain dump of everything you do on a regular basis. It may surprise you to see what you actually do, or you may struggle to remember where all your time goes. If that is the case, you may want to do a time audit for two weeks to really track where exactly your time goes.

2. **What *should* I do?** Once you have created a list of what you do, circle or star those tasks that only you can do. The default answer for most people to this question is . . . everything. But really push yourself to answer this question honestly. Don't settle for being like most people. Redefine your normal by being willing to let other people help you get things done.

3. **What should someone else do?** You should delegate everything left on your list to someone else. Everything. That doesn't mean you can delegate all of it right away. You may need to add the right people, do more training, or create processes and procedures for other people to follow so they know what to do. But don't let the pursuit of perfection stop you from delegating all those tasks. If you can train someone else to do something anywhere close to 80 percent as well as you can, delegate it.

If you're wondering what your best next move should be, listen to Rachel Rodgers. Rachel is an accomplished entrepreneur and CEO and co-founder of Hello Seven. She has made it her mission to teach women and marginalized communities to build wealth. When we were talking about the best first step to take when learning the art of delegation, she told me the most important lesson was this: *Get a personal assistant as soon as you possibly can.*

If you can afford to pay somebody twenty hours a week or five hours a week, as soon as you can eke out a part of your budget for that—*absolutely* do it. Because as soon as you start learning how to delegate to somebody else, how to explain something to somebody else, you're going to learn leadership skills you need to run a team later.

It is so crucial to start learning those skills of how to lead others, how to delegate to others, how to communicate, and how to support the person working for your company.[1]

I couldn't agree more. My own delegation skills really took off about six months after I launched *The School of Greatness* show. My method of operations was, to put it mildly, chaotic. I'm the creative guy who is always eager to jump into that next big thing and hope someone else is taking care of the details. That's when Sarah Livingstone, my incredible personal assistant, entered my life, and she has been with me for over a decade!

Organization wasn't a strength of mine. But it is one of hers. She immediately helped me address my chaotic personal space and supported me in so many ways—optimizing day-to-day tasks, taking charge of my calendar, and holding me accountable for what I was doing. Sarah tackled a giant of a job with grace and efficiency. If anything, I may have delegated too much too quickly to keep up with everything that was going on at the time. But she handled it all without missing a beat.

Thankfully, she's still an integral part of the Greatness team and still assists me. I could not have done what I have been able to do without her support. It's comforting to know she's always looking out for me as a supportive member of our team. And I have learned so much from her as she has helped me grow in so many ways.

DELEGATE RUTHLESSLY

Another person to whom I have delegated a great deal is Matt Cesaratto. Matt joined the team not long after Sarah when I realized I needed someone else to manage and lead the day-to-day operations of Greatness Media. It was the classic dilemma: I struggled to be the visionary and the talent for the show while also managing the team and teaching them processes. Plus, my natural strengths didn't position me to focus on operations.

I brought in Matt, my long-time friend from college, to help us scale and grow. I knew I could delegate things to him and trust that he would get them done. In turn, I empowered him to hire, train, and further delegate to the team. Delegating to Matt freed me to do even more of what only I can do. The result has been a close working relationship borne out of both a 10-year friendship and almost a decade of working together in the trenches to build Greatness Media.

I love how Matt described the dynamic of the working relationship the three of us share. "Lewis brings the fire—he's the visionary. Sarah brings the rocks around the campfire—she protects and supports him. I bring the kindling and stoke the fire—I help the fire burn brighter. We truly care about each other. We're a part of each other's lives. We're committed to this path."

Without Sarah and Matt, I would have been limited to my own skills and talents. And we would never have maximized the mission, because they have kept this mission from becoming a mess. They helped me find the right people and empower the team with a culture of delegation. As a team we keep building upward—together.

When we talked about delegation, Matt shared these four best practices for effective delegation:

1. **Identify the things only you can do and delegate everything else.** Be honest about your strengths and weaknesses. Be clear about the things that are the highest-value components of what you do, and delegate the rest. People want to feel invested in a vision or organization, so openly share your vision when you find people whose strengths are your weaknesses. Provide support without reinventing your processes and systems—use good systems, structures, and rigor. When in doubt, ask your team members what they need to do their job effectively and efficiently. Above all, be willing to let go of almost everything.

2. **Stay flexible.** A growing organization will shift and change in ways you may not expect. But if you and your team are too rigid, it gets difficult to adapt so you can grow and scale. When you bring on new people, make sure they understand your vision and culture. Realize that it's important to get comfortable with being uncomfortable. As a perk, the change that comes from growth keeps your job from becoming a boring routine.

3. **Budget for experts.** Instead of looking at yourself as a solopreneur, envision yourself as a true business.

Set aside money for the expertise you need, or you will likely pay for it later. Things like legal advice, accounting, training, tools, social media management—it's worth having the money to spend on the things that don't light you up so you have the time to spend on the parts of your business you do love to do.

4. **Know your numbers. They never lie.** Ignorance is not bliss when it comes to money! Create a financial structure that gives you a data-derived template you can use to make sensible decisions. No one ever wants to question the personal integrity of a team member. And if keeping track of finances isn't your strength, find someone you can trust. Work together to develop a system that makes discussing the numbers an easy, objective conversation on a regular basis. Have regularly scheduled meetings to update one another on financial matters. Don't just ignore the numbers until something pops up that doesn't make sense to you. You want money conversations to be incredibly boring, never surprising.

For me, I've learned that the best question to ask yourself at the beginning of the day isn't *What will I have to get done or fix today?* Instead, the best questions are:

- *How do I help make a great team even better?*
- *How do I build a better-integrated culture so everyone feels connected without me?*
- *How can we get better at reaching and serving more people?*

I get excited about delegating to the team because I know they are what will get us to our Meaningful Mission of touching 100 million lives a week. When you have a culture that is ready to delegate ruthlessly, people don't hold on too tightly. They get their jobs done well without rashly delegating too quickly. As a result, they move as a unit and are equipped to overcome whatever comes their way.

When you mobilize your team, you unlock their greatest potential.

— Lewis Howes

MOBILIZE YOUR TEAM

It's ironic how, deep down, most of us fear delegating because we don't want to lose control. We want to keep our hands on the wheel. The only person we trust to get the job done is ourself. But when we take that perspective, we miss this counterintuitive truth: delegation is a source of security. Delegation allows us to have security we otherwise would never have because we are strengthening our areas of weakness, those places where we might otherwise have become vulnerable. When people don't think in terms of delegation, they often fail to investigate options that might be of great help to them. They dismiss those options casually, thinking that what they don't already know can't be of much value. But the opposite is often true. It's what we don't yet know or understand that opens possibilities for us.

On the other hand, simply pursuing something that is difficult in order to prove something to yourself isn't a wise move either. Chasing after everything can leave you spread too thin and vulnerable in a variety of ways. Don't dismiss what you don't yet know, and don't feel like you have to prove yourself to anyone.

Remember this core truth from *The Greatness Mindset*: you are enough, and you are becoming more. Enjoy the journey.

When you mobilize your team, you unlock your team's greatest potential. Every person can be an incredible asset. The people on my team bring their own diverse talents and skills. Their specific gifts are not the same as mine—and I love it! It can be easy to think that if the whole team were just more like me, then we would get more done. After all, the easiest trap of all is when we start to think, *If only my team worked as hard as I did all the time, then we would see results.* That kind of thinking only results in the whole team burying themselves under the weight of your expectations. If you are working too hard and expect your team to work as hard as you, all you will end up with is a team of exhausted people worn out by an improper work-life balance.

Maybe you need to stop telling your team what to do and start empowering them to do what they do best. Often their unique abilities will cover your weak spots. For example, if I were to try to juggle what Sarah, Matt, and I all do, then the only thing I would produce is a mess. They can do their stuff much better than I can.

Here are the five keys I've learned to help mobilize my own team through the Mobility Habit:

1. **Know your mission.** To do this you need to start with yourself. What's your intention behind your Meaningful Mission? Why do you have the money goals you have? Personal fulfillment, financial peace, making a positive impact, or maybe a combination of the above?

   Whatever your vision is, your ability to express these plans openly and effectively with your team will give them a chance to decide early on whether they align with it. It's okay if some people are on a different path from yours. If it doesn't work out long term, don't try to hold on too tightly. Let the teammate relationship go, but keep a professional relationship in place. Again, there's no point in unenrolling someone just because they are no longer on your team.

2. **Set meaningful goals.** Be willing to work with your team to establish meaningful goals that everyone can work toward. Take the initiative to start the conversations. Discuss why those goals are important. Explore what this enterprise means to each person, both personally and professionally, so that when challenges come up, you can help each other move forward.

   There will be twists and turns, but when you know the people who are helping you build this dream, you can lean on each other for support and grow closer together through adversity. Over time, that trust will pay off when you reach your summit together.

3. **Tap into your self-awareness.** Identify the skills necessary to achieve the goals you created. Acknowledge which areas are your strengths and

which are your weaknesses. Think about soft skills like communication, leadership, and emotional intelligence, as well as hard skills such as technical expertise and industry knowledge. Consider finding ways to boost your weaker areas, and encourage your team to list their strengths and weaknesses as well.

4. **Communicate well.** In delegation, communication is key. Your team needs you to set clear expectations and provide regular, timely feedback. You may need to create training videos so they can learn the quality of work you expect. People on your team aren't mind readers, as cool as that would be. They don't know what you want unless you explain it. But before you spend all your time teaching each person one-on-one, create a set of procedures and expectations for each process and system instead.

   If laying out the details isn't your strength, work with a team member who loves digging into all the details of how things should work. Talk them through your ideal guidelines and have them ask questions for clarity along the way.

   Train the people who will be responsible for each specific task and document everything. Isn't this a lot of work? Yes, but it really is worth it in the end. You won't have to explain and re-explain things to people, and they won't feel like they don't have enough information to do what you ask of them. Keep the lines of communication open, and reevaluate those processes and systems as needed. If a team member has a more efficient way to complete a task, empower them to share their suggestions and update the documentation.

   Feedback is important for your team so they know what they are doing well and what they can improve. When the processes and systems are clearly established, it will be easier for them to own their daily responsibilities. Encourage an environment of personal growth and continuous learning. Take some time to celebrate wins, offer constructive feedback, and regularly identify areas for improvement.

5. **Equip your team to get results.** When you delegate, you can't ignore the results. You need shared, healthy accountability by tracking results on a weekly or daily basis to ensure everyone is on course. And you will need to make course corrections based on that data. If you simply ask someone to do something and come back in a month to check on progress, you'll be disappointed most of the time. When you create shared expectations and then set them up for success, you'll see consistently better results.

   For example, they may need help in the form of an outside consultant, special training, a course, a book, or other tools to deliver the results you want. If you want to truly harness the power of delegating, you'll need to continuously invest in training for your people, especially as today's workplace constantly evolves. Long gone are the days when someone could learn how to run one machine in a factory and be set for life. The global marketplace shifts constantly, and your team will need to be nimble and adapt to it. Equip them and they'll thank you by delivering better results.

The bottom line is this: You cannot expect to do it all alone. One person cannot do everything. You need to learn to delegate if you want to grow and scale. Every top business owner in the world got where they are because they were able to let go of what they needed to in order to pursue what they wanted.

Remember, if you want something done right, by all means, do it yourself. But if you want to do something great, do it with others.

YOUR GAME PLAN

Exercise 1: The Two-Week Time Audit

Before you can delegate things, you must know where your time is going. The two-week time audit will help you see exactly where you spend your time and discover which tasks can be automated or delegated. Start by searching online for a weekly template with 15-minute time blocks. Print it and keep it handy. Every hour, write how you spent your time for the preceding blocks of time. Do this as accurately as possible for two weeks.

When the two weeks are up, categorize your blocks of time. It may help to create color-coded labels that correspond to your blocks, such as:

- Administrative tasks
- Checking email
- Meetings
- Client calls
- Creative work
- Sales calls
- Recording podcasts
- Writing social posts
- Training

Once you've created your own list and organized your time, it's time to see what can be eliminated (time wasters), automated (time robbers), and delegated (time savers). Now that you are armed with this information, ruthlessly eliminate tasks and activities that you shouldn't be doing.

Exercise 2: Unlock the Strengths of Your Team

We often hire people because they can perform specific roles but never dive deeper into their capabilities and strengths. This exercise will help you look at your team in a new way and make sure they are positioned to operate at their best. When you do this well, it also frees you up to delegate more effectively.

To begin, make a list of everyone on your team. Use the questions below to reflect on what they can and should be doing and, more importantly, where they have untapped potential that you can access:

- What are their core strengths?
- What are their weaknesses or challenges?
- What is their current capacity or workload?
- What types of things do they enjoy? (Where do they come alive as they work?)
- In what areas have you noticed them shining in their work?
- What gifts do they have in your organization that make them stand out from the rest?
- What talents have you seen in them?
- What skills do they have that may not be tied to their role?
- What is their personality or wiring?
- Where do you see them going beyond what is expected of them in their role?

As you work through these questions, try to get a sense of the whole person. Then do some creative thinking. Start with a blank slate and imagine that you are building your team from scratch. Based on what you now know about each team member, are they in the right seats? What would your team look like in this reimagined state? Are there moves you can make now to make it happen?

The aim of this exercise isn't to blow up your organization. Rather, it's to position you to always be looking for ways to unlock the potential of your people and put them in the best place to thrive.

CHAPTER TWELVE

HABIT 7: THE MASTERY HABIT

Cultivate Your Money Wisdom

We have a financial literacy problem. It isn't only that so many of us don't know much about money; we don't even know what we don't know. And it shows. More than three in four Americans say they live paycheck to paycheck.[1] Another one in four say they haven't saved anything for retirement,[2] and at least one in five don't have emergency savings.[3]

Unfortunately, most of us simply weren't instructed about how to be wise with money. Not only do we not understand how to have a healthy relationship with it, but we also just aren't taught what to do with it at all. We are expected to either wing it or figure it out somewhere between high school and college. And we aren't given the tools to prepare us to pay our own taxes, understand how to avoid credit card debt, or properly invest our money.

Money plays an important role in securing a safe and comfortable life, but without the proper tools and training, people end up stuck. From an early age, kids learn most of what they do know about money from their parents. But if the family treats money as a "hush-hush" topic of conversation like it was in my family, then kids go into the world unaware of what money can do *to* or *for* them.

Too many people today are drowning in debt because no one taught kids how to swim in the financial literacy pool. Some parents have extensive experience in the financial world and teach their children what they know; they are the Olympic swimmers who train their kids in technique and proper form. But not everyone has access to that expertise. Many parents are still trying to understand for themselves how to create a healthy relationship with money. The resulting lack of substantive conversations around money is one of the main reasons why so many in our country struggle with financial peace. Financial literacy—or the Mastery Habit—is critical to discovering and enjoying financial peace.

WHY WE DON'T TALK ABOUT MONEY

If you want to make money easy, you must grow your money wisdom. While money is something everyone interacts with every day, we don't talk about it the same way we do about the weather. We don't overhear people discussing their portfolios in a coffee shop or chatting about monthly payments. We don't hear people talking openly about how much it costs to do the things they love to do. It's a taboo topic.

Think about it: How often have you felt able to ask hard questions and speak freely about your financial situation? If your answer is close to never, you aren't alone. It's normal to discuss topics about which we feel confident and knowledgeable. We don't naturally want to join conversations in which we don't feel confident. So we don't talk about money as much because we simply don't know much about it. And we don't want other people to know that we don't know.

Maybe you grew up in a family that meant well but projected a poor image of finances. Maybe the conversations, body language, and energy about money always left you feeling negative. As a result, you've never thought about money in a positive way.

But here's the thing: You can't attract more of something good in your life if you are afraid to discuss it. Money comes to you when you are ready for it, but it rarely comes to you if you can't talk about it with positivity. Once I realized I had negative energy surrounding my conversations about money, everything started to open up for me.

It used to surprise me when folks I had on the show would ask me about my money. I always felt like I was being put under a microscope to discuss my finances in front of my entire audience. But it helped me overcome my fear of talking about money. Over time it became natural, and I wasn't afraid to discuss it anymore. And I realized that the more people I had on the show who shared their knowledge about money, the more my viewership went up. Clearly, people wanted to join in the conversation.

Is there someone in your life who is comfortable talking with you about money? It can be a friend, family member, peer, or mentor. If you know some people who've never discussed money around you, ask them why. Don't be afraid to ask if they'd be interested in having more money conversations.

START THE CONVERSATION

One of the best ways to learn is to ask questions. Ask people who may know more than you do how they see money. Seek to learn from the best and apply what you learn. See what works and what doesn't. If you are willing to ask questions, you can get serious about mastering money.

Here are a few simple starter questions you can ask to increase your number of money conversations. To avoid misunderstandings, I would frame these questions by saying something like, "I'm on a journey to learn more about how to manage money, so I'm talking more about money with people I can learn from. Can I ask you a few questions?"

Then start with some of the following questions:

- What percentage of your income do you put toward your monthly expenses, and why?

- How much money do you set aside to save each month?

- What are the things you like to save money for, and why?

- Do you invest money? Where do you invest it, and why?

- How much do you set aside to give to others or support causes you care about?

- What is one thing you wish someone had told you about money when you were younger?

- What is something you have been learning about money recently?

These are only conversation-starter questions, of course, and you should feel free to create your own. When you find people who can help you talk freely about money, you will start learning more about how it can work for you, along with challenging your own Money Story.

Don't just settle for talking about money. Like most things in life, if you want something to expand, you must invest in it. This investment could be money, time, energy, or a combination of the three. When you're willing to put yourself out there and do the research, study, learn, and find the sources you resonate with, you're on the right path to financial literacy.

It's never a bad bet when you invest in yourself. Whether you can invest a lot or a little in your financial education, there are plenty of resources out there that you can make part of your learning routine, such as:

- Masterminds

- Membership sites

- Books

- Digital courses

- YouTube videos

- Podcasts

- Blogs

- Meetups

- Forums

- Conferences

It's never a
bad bet when
you invest
in yourself.

— Lewis Howes

The more you learn, the more confident you'll feel about sharing new information and ideas with others. By sharing the things you're learning about money, you can spark an interest among those around you. As momentum grows, negative thoughts about money conversations will get replaced with curiosity and great questions as more of your friends and family members let go of the stigma around talking about money.

I take the concept of lifelong learning to heart. It's a key to my success. Year after year I invest in coaches to help me improve in the areas I feel are important based on my interests during different seasons of my life. At any given time, I'll have a coach for working out. I've had a Spanish coach to help me master a new language. I have a therapist, business mentors, financial advisors, and many other coaches.

I'm always investing in new ways to learn and grow because I feel like I'm regressing if I'm not improving my knowledge base and growing my skill sets. That's why you'll always see me taking notes on my show. I'm always hungry to learn.

QUESTION PAST ADVICE

Financial guru Dave Ramsey went from establishing a $4 million real estate portfolio as a 26-year-old to filing for bankruptcy and losing everything by age 30. In a one-on-one, he told me how that experience made him feel: "Pain is a thorough teacher. It was a rich time. The fertilizer was everywhere—lots of places to grow stuff."[4]

That mindset is profound. When things hit the fan, looking at the experience as an opportunity for growth is the perspective of a student learning from their teacher. So many people let their past mistakes and misconceptions decide their future understanding of money. They allow their history with money to be an excuse. Others try to avoid responsibility by placing the blame, guilt, or shame from that misconception onto the person who first shared those beliefs with them. This only leads to a dead end. You have to be willing to confront the lies from your past to grow into your richer future.

Jaspreet Singh is the creator of the Minority Mindset, an attorney, an investor, and CEO of both *Market Briefs* and *Market Insider*. He has joined me on *The School of Greatness* several times. Jaspreet has made it his mission to make financial education both fun and accessible. He has helped countless people get out of debt, start investing, and create a plan for building wealth.

Jaspreet told me he has found three common lies that are the easiest to fall for:

Lie #1: You need to have a college degree to become wealthy.

If you take out student loans to get a college degree, you graduate with debt instead of wealth. Even though some degrees advertise that their students will be starting out with a six-figure salary, those same students are working hard to pay off their debt. Out of the gate, their expected income doesn't align with their reality. These former students try to manage a lifestyle that they think should reflect the job they have.

The reality is, just because you work for a Fortune 500 company or have your graduate or postgraduate degree, doesn't mean your debt evaporates. Of course, I'm not saying all school debt is bad. I'm only pointing out that you can't simply assume a degree guarantees more money. Be strategic about your learning path.

Lie #2: Your main goal should be to climb the corporate ladder.

There is a traffic jam on the corporate ladder. If you can climb the corporate ladder while also building a ladder of your own, you're likely to better position yourself for long-term success. Putting all your bets on one path to success doesn't usually go the way you think it will. In business, anything is possible, and you can't prepare for every contingency.

Does that mean giving up? Not at all! But it does mean that you should probably plan to build an alternative route to success. If you lose your corporate job, you lose the income that went with it. But if you're using some of your income to create your own business, you can grow something that belongs to you.

Lie #3: A savings account is a good investment.

If you just park your cash in a low-interest savings account, you give the bank money to invest. You effectively get next to nothing in return. The bank is not going to invest in you. They will invest your money, but you won't see the return on that investment. If you build your own investment portfolio and put your money in that, then you give money a chance to work for *you* instead of for the bank. I don't have a problem with banks. But I prefer to know that while I'm working to earn money, my money is also working on the side to help me with my mission.

Maybe you've heard some of these lies before in your own Money Story. If so, please understand the people who gave you this advice were only trying to help. Most likely it is the same advice they once received.

The goal here isn't to call people out for spreading misinformation but to help you see that you don't have to continue following and sharing the same advice *if it no longer serves you*. It's about looking at the things you've learned and deciding what still feels relevant and what you can let go of to make space for new information, ideas, and beliefs.

THE FINANCIAL KNOWLEDGE FLOW

It's not about you. That is how Rick Warren began his best-selling book *The Purpose Driven Life*. And the same is true when you want to acquire more money wisdom.

As counterintuitive as it may seem, if you want to live a richer, more abundant life, you can't just strive to get more knowledge for your own use. You need to think about how your knowledge can serve the people around you. Ironically, by thinking of others as you grow your know-how, you actually position yourself to make more money.

I call it the Financial Knowledge Flow. It looks like this:

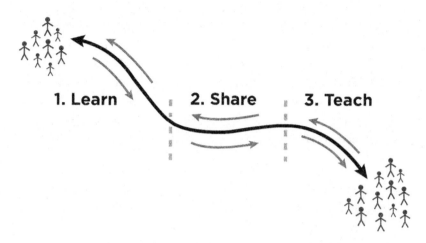

Phase 1: Learn. *Reach up* to others who know more than you do. You can get some of this knowledge through books, interviews, podcasts, and other media, but you'll also want access to financial mentors who can increase your own financial literacy levels. If you think you will learn everything on your own, you'll take longer and miss a lot of things you could have learned from others' wins and mistakes. And as you learn, you have more wisdom to . . .

Phase 2: Share. *Lean on* others who are in a similar place as you on your money journey. Share what you have learned in your own life to encourage, support, and lift one another to reach the next level. Being generous with what you have learned not only helps make the world a better place but also positions you as a go-to source of valuable info. As your network grows, so will your reputation for financial wisdom and you can begin to . . .

Phase 3: Teach. *Invest in* others who can benefit from what you learn. Don't forget that the best way to truly learn is to teach others what you have learned. Seek ways to teach what you learn to people who perhaps don't have access to your connections or haven't had the same opportunities you enjoy. Don't forget to look down and lift up others as you climb. You can always find someone who doesn't yet know what you have learned.

This practice stems from Habit 1, the Mindset Habit (Chapter 6) of being generous with what you have to help raise up others as you go. And as you teach, you reengage the process and begin to learn from those you teach who bring fresh perspectives and insights to you.

As you learn, share, and teach, you increase the Financial Knowledge Flow. As the momentum increases, it will keep lifting up others and propelling you forward as well.

SEVEN LESSONS FROM BABYLON

One of the most influential books on wealth ever written is *The Richest Man in Babylon* by George Samuel Clason. Whether I'm talking to millionaires, billionaires, or casual investors, this book often comes up when we discuss wealth, money, and investing. People have used its principles for many years as a guiding light for building long-term wealth.

The book shares seven key lessons. Since it was written as a parable in 1926, I'm going to modernize the concepts and add insights I've received from interviewing my guests over the years.

1. **Pay yourself first.** During the safety demonstrations on airplanes, the flight attendants tell you, "Put on your own oxygen mask first before attempting to help others." But when it comes to money, you may want to pay others first. You give that gift to your partner or buy that new pair of shoes for a friend before you save money for yourself. Instead, you first need to make sure your cup is full so you can then start pouring into someone else's. David Bach, a financial expert and 10-time *New York Times* best-selling author, puts it this way: "First, we need to make a promise to ourselves to become financially selfish and focus on our own financial goals before anyone else's."[5]

Start by setting aside a percentage of what you make into your savings or investments to set yourself up for the future. This way, you proactively prepare yourself financially for unexpected situations that may arise. How much money should you put away? David suggests setting aside one hour's worth of what you earn per day. So if you earn $100 during a 10-hour workday, set $10 aside.

Shark Tank investor and serial entrepreneur Kevin O'Leary says we should set aside 10 percent of every penny we make—no questions asked. My advice to people who are trying to build a business or achieve a big-time goal is you can go as slowly as you want, but just don't stop. Do whatever you can when it comes to savings, but make the commitment to stick to it.

Tony Robbins says to think of your savings as a tax being charged that you have no control over. Pretend like it's gone forever—and just gets "paid" to you every single month. Automating this amount makes it even easier for you to ignore the account where it's piling up month after month.

2. **Control your expenses.** This is a big one—living within your means is such an easily overlooked but vitally important lesson. You could blame the Instagram lifestyle, society's obsession with materialistic things, or a bunch of other factors. But the truth is, overspending and not managing your expenses have always been problems.

   People who aren't used to having money spend too much too quickly once it hits their hands. You see it a lot with pro athletes and celebrities, but it also happens with just about anyone who gets some extra cash. It's exciting to see money coming in, and it feels cool to reward yourself by spending it.

   Living within your means starts with setting a spending plan and sticking to it. Whether you make $30,000 or $3 million, learning to manage your expenses—knowing what you can spend and where you can spend it—creates a cornerstone on which you can build long-term wealth. Billionaire and legendary investor Ray Dalio says the first step to controlling your expenses and budgeting is to figure out how much you have saved and how long those savings will last if you lose all your sources of income. Then decide how much you want to grow that amount.

Let's say you have enough savings to last three months with no other income, but you want to have two years' worth instead. Calculate how much you need to set aside per paycheck or per month to reach that goal. Once you have a number in mind, automate it.

With all the technology out there, you can use apps to help you see where you're spending your money. They can even help you set goals to save for a trip or a big purchase instead of swiping a credit card and not having the money to pay it off when the bill comes.

3. **Make your money multiply.** Another mentor of mine, Tony Robbins, wrote a number one *New York Times* bestseller called *Money: Master the Game.* He says the worst exchange in the world is trading time for money. It's better to maximize the money you're making and figure out how to multiply it in different ways.

No matter how much or how little you make, hourly wages will always have an earning ceiling because you can only be in one place at one time. If you're the highest-paid consultant in your industry, you still should figure out a way to generate passive income with the money you're making.

There are ways to multiply your money even if you aren't able to invest in higher-ticket assets like real estate or franchising. Once you have your savings situated, you may want to learn about investing in stocks, bonds, IRAs, index funds, mutual funds, or even a 401k. Ray Dalio got his start in the stock market when he was really young by investing the spare money he earned by caddying on a golf course.

Just like working on your savings, the most important thing to remember when trying to make your money multiply is to make a plan and follow through with it consistently.

4. **Protect your money from losses.** This one can be tricky because for entrepreneurs, a willingness to take risks comes with the territory. When it comes to building long-term wealth, we need to approach money differently. Ramit Sethi, author of *I Will Teach*

You to Be Rich and founder of the organization by the same name, is a master when it comes to the stock market and investing. Something he said really surprised me: Ramit only checks his portfolio about once per month. This helps him avoid making reactive decisions based on where the market is on any given day. It helps him avoid buying something just because it's hot and focus instead on more secure, stable, long-term investments. Since all of Ramit's accounts are automated, he doesn't have to think about where his money is going. He can sit back and let the long game work in his favor.

Diversifying your portfolio is another great strategy for reducing risk. I know it's fun to make daily trades and try to beat the system. But the reality is, some of the world's largest firms spend hundreds of millions of dollars on market research. It's just not a fair fight, so the best way to increase your chances of investments panning out is to not put all your eggs in one basket.

This doesn't mean you can't have some fun with Bitcoin, crypto, or other less stable investments. Ramit and I have acted as angel investors over the years, and though neither of us earned our money back, we had a lot of fun. We approached it as a gamble instead of an investment for more future money. When it comes to taking financial risks, don't invest more money than you can afford to lose.

5. **Own your home.** This one is debatable nowadays. There are some people who say you shouldn't own your home right away because you should take that big chunk of money and invest it in yourself first or maybe in another asset that earns more interest and creates cash flow. Then once you have another level of savings and an income, you can own your home.

    But we've all heard the importance of owning your home, condo, or apartment as a stable asset that usually increases in value over time. Dave Ramsey talks a lot about this, but the principle doesn't only apply to real estate. It can also apply to business investments. You want to understand where you are when it comes to owning your home, but you want to "own your home" by investing in yourself.

Whatever industry or career you're in, aim for some type of ownership. It could include taking the opportunity to monetize your skill set, being part of a company, or building your own company on the side. And if you're in a position at work where you can get a stake, some shares, or some equity, that would be an effective way to do this. If you own a business, it could mean investing money back into the company to help it grow faster and further.

Even if you aren't in one of those positions right now, we all have the opportunity to become partial owners of a company through the stock market. David Bach told me that there are only two escalators to building long-term wealth—real estate and the stock market. If you haven't already, empower yourself by starting small and building up your portfolio to increase your long-term investments. It's all about accumulating wealth over time.

Don't invest more money than you can afford to lose.

— Lewis Howes

6. **Ensure a future income.** This doesn't necessarily mean you have to try to get a million followers on Instagram or become TikTok famous. Following this lesson could be as simple as creating a website to showcase your designs if you're a graphic designer and networking with other designers in your local area at meetups, conferences, or events. If you're a business coach, it could mean posting videos on YouTube showcasing your expertise.

   I won't lie to you and say numbers don't matter at all, but they're not the most important part. Publishing content that's aligned with your personal brand shows your passion and could set you up for future success. It allows others to see that you care about the work you do.

   Everything published online is a résumé nowadays. Be productive and proactive by building your personal brand through it. Don't rob the world of your talents! Be proud of the work you do and showcase the gifts you were given. It might not seem like you're doing much in the short term, but believe me, it's one of the best things you can do for yourself to really ensure your future income is guaranteed and recession proof.

   Launching a side hustle by using your nights and weekends to build up another source of revenue might potentially provide a financial cushion and give you more money to add to your investments. About one in three people in the U.S. has a side business, and others are making plans to start one soon. You're in good company if you're planning a side hustle right now.

7. **Increase your ability to earn.** If you're already running a business or side hustle, you could start by simply increasing your rates. This can allow you to make more while potentially working less. It gets easier as you gain more experience and recognition in your industry. Of course, more products lead to

more potential sales for your business. Just make sure they add value and solve a real pain point for your customers.

Another way to increase your ability to earn is to expand your reach and get more leads with your marketing and advertising. Think critically about your target audience and the platforms they're using. Decide the kind of content you can create on that platform and the content you can create and package into a webinar, E-book, or online course.

As you grow, you can increase efficiency by creating repeatable systems and workflows that automate and optimize your processes. When people on your team can understand how to complete tasks more efficiently and find answers to their questions within your systems, it frees up more time for you to focus on more important tasks.

Finally, having an experienced and dedicated team is one of the best investments you can ever make for your business. It will buy back your time, allow you to focus on what you're good at, and help pave the way for exponential growth.

LEARN MORE TO EARN MORE

If you want to earn more, you need to learn more. The ability to learn can turn any situation into a win. I've made a lot of mistakes on my own money journey and learned a lot from those mistakes. For example, back when I first tried out angel investing, I quite frankly knew nothing about investing.

If you want to earn more, you need to learn more.

— Lewis Howes

Without doing any research, I invested $25,000. Then I made seven or eight more investments, some as high as $50,000. At one point I even put in $100,000. In the 10 years since, I've gotten pretty much zero return on those investments.

Looking back, I wouldn't call it a waste. It was one of the clearest lessons I ever learned about investing. Don't go in blind, or you'll get blindsided. Learning that lesson made the experience worthwhile.

If I hadn't gotten involved in that kind of investment, I wouldn't have learned the dos and don'ts of that industry. I also learned how to cut my losses and reevaluate my options. I needed to learn what to invest in, who to invest with, what partners I would need, and why angel investing is so risky in general.

Could I have learned it without losing all that money? Of course. But I didn't know what I didn't know. That situation gave me the fertile opportunity to grow in financial literacy, plus it gave me a story to share to help keep others from making the same mistakes.

Today I'm comfortable with taking longer to make decisions. I don't feel rushed when something is trending. I assess, get feedback, and seek out the best people in that field so I can learn more from their experiences before taking a risk myself.

Of course, I didn't learn that right away, especially back when I first heard about the new thing called cryptocurrency. Once again, people thought it was the next big thing and were really excited about it. I barely knew what it was but thought, *Maybe they're right. I should get on this.* I barely did any research and dropped $100,000 into it. Essentially, I made the same mistake twice: I didn't learn more but still expected to earn more.

I set myself up for financial hardship, stress, and disappointment. I got emotional about my loss and with myself because I felt I should have seen it coming. But the reality is, I'm human. I learned that even a loss that big is not the end of the world.

Sure, I was disappointed. But I knew I would be okay. That was a lesson in itself: I could afford to make mistakes. Maybe not all the time, but when I did make them, I could survive and learn from them.

Since then, I've tried all kinds of investment opportunities and learned a lot in doing so. Each market is different. As I progress in my money journey, I learn more with each one. For example, the real estate market has been a constant one. People generally see property as a good investment. It consistently brings value to people over time, generates great returns, and will always be in demand. But that doesn't mean it doesn't have risks. Anyone who lived through the 2008 financial crisis can tell you that.

I started studying the real estate market using the lessons I learned from my turbulent investment career. I read books cover to cover. I kept up with market trends in the news. I reached out to experts and interviewed them. Anyone selling single-family houses, condos, agricultural land, or even people renting, hosting an Airbnb, or subleasing had unique insider information for me.

I learned all I could so I could maximize my earning potential. I learned how to read the market. It became a kind of hobby because I enjoyed doing it so much. Becoming familiar with what people want in their prospective property made the subject relatable to me because I love working with people, adding value, and building things to help them achieve their potential.

I took the time to grow, understand, and listen to those who had already made the mistakes. To put it simply—I studied. Then I started investing by placing small amounts into real estate funds that could minimize risk and grow over time. Unlike with crypto, I didn't drop $100,000 into the first opportunity.

My initial real estate investments proved to be valuable. For the first time in my life, I had consistent monthly revenue coming in from my investments. The more real estate proved to me that it was worth my money, the more I trusted it. Almost like a relationship, the industry had to earn my trust for me to want to give. I had to know there would be a way to control and minimize the risk.

I used to treat my investments like speed dating. I would go all in and hope it worked out. But that's not how healthy relationships grow. A strong relationship needs a solid foundation. It takes time, thought, and intention to help it survive the test of time.

I didn't have this mindset as a kid, teen, or even young adult. I assumed it would all go my way. That mindset got the better of me and taught me a lesson. Then my experiences of being too hasty with investing reinforced that lesson. Now I'm able to use that education to better understand money.

The more you know, the more you can grow. That is why the Mastery Habit must become part of your life routine, the critical capstone habit that all the other habits support. I had to learn more to earn more. And so do you.

YOUR GAME PLAN

Exercise 1: Identify Your Own Money Lies

Before you can engage the Mastery Habit, you have to get rid of the lies that hold you back. If you have a voice in your head saying money is bad or fleeting or evil, you'll never master your money. Begin by going back to your Money Story and reflecting on any lies that may be buried inside it. Some of these may be buried deep and painful to dig up, but it will be worth it. Once you've written them out and can see the lies for what they are, write a corresponding truth to replace the lie.

Here are the prompts to have an honest conversation with yourself about your money lies:

- I believe . . .
- I feel . . .
- I think . . .
- I worry about . . .
- I avoid . . .

For example, you might write:

I feel no matter how hard I work, I'll never have enough money. But the truth is, my needs are met, and I have a gift to share with the world. I will use my time wisely and build a side business that allows me to share my gift with others and, in the process, receive a rich financial reward.

It will take a bit of work to believe the truth, but keep coming back to it for as long as it takes to reach mastery.

Exercise 2: Learn from the Best

I've been privileged to speak with some of the greatest money experts in the world on *The School of Greatness*, and I want to challenge you to learn from them, just as I have. Add these episodes to your queue, and over the next two weeks, binge-listen or watch them all. Take notes. Learn well. Share with others. And teach the lessons. This will help you internalize their wisdom and lead you to mastering the Mastery Habit.

- Jaspreet Singh
- Dean Graziosi
- Alex Hormozi
- Rachel Rodgers
- Ray Dalio
- Dave Ramsey
- Tony Robbins
- Grant Cardone
- Rory Vaden
- Ramit Sethi
- Bob Proctor
- Joe Dispenza
- Gino Wickman
- Ken Honda
- Patrick Bet-David
- Chris Guillebeau
- Daymond John
- Barbara Corcoran
- Jen Sincero

Note: Your story is unique to you, so remember that the advice given in these episodes are the opinions of the speakers and not guaranteed strategies for financial success.

CONCLUSION

Let's Do This!

You made it! By finishing this book, you've shown that you are serious about changing the direction of your Money Story for the better.

I hope the lessons in these pages have been as helpful to you as they have been for me over the years. I'm sure you're excited to get started, but before you begin living your new Money Story and enjoying your healthier relationship with money, I hope you will take a moment to reflect on how far you've already come.

- How have your feelings toward money changed?
- How have you felt encouraged throughout this part of your journey?
- Where did you experience healing from your past?
- Where do you think you still need to do more healing work?
- What habits resonated most with you?

The lessons in this book are only the first chapter in your new Money Story. It takes daily discipline to reinforce these habits in your life. I know from experience. Every morning, I reorient myself around these habits and make it my goal to constantly live on mission.

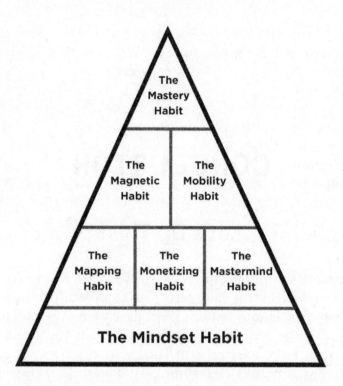

I've prepared a short assessment for you to evaluate the health of your relationship with money now, but first, one of the most important things you can do now is to reconnect with each of the 7 Money Habits on a regular basis.

Habit 1: The Mindset Habit: Live Generously

I encourage you to intentionally return to Habit 1 every day. Make it a point to say something you're grateful for and think about that thing. Actively consider how you can better show your gratitude to and for others. Make that your last thought before your head hits the pillow. That way you start each day refreshed and ready with a heart full of gratitude.

It isn't always easy. Sometimes you may have to be reminded to be grateful. But it makes a world of difference. Living with gratitude and a positive mindset each day prepares you for everything that follows and multiplies all the other habits.

Habit 2: The Mapping Habit: Plan Your Life

If you never map out your future, you'll tend to retrace your past. You can live life without retracing your past mistakes when you stay focused on your future plans. Living out this habit means you're constantly running toward your goals. Take the lessons you learn along the way and leave the rest behind. Always strive to know where you are and where you are going.

By refusing to live in the past, you keep yourself from being controlled by it. When you drive yourself forward, you're better able to project your vision for others to see. Plus, by making a plan and sticking to it, you are able to recover from setbacks faster. You learn where you got off track and how to pursue your goals with that same passion that got you started. Then you are well-positioned to plan your rich day, rich year, and an even richer life.

Habit 3: The Monetizing Habit: Appreciate Your Value

The way you choose to live brings you closer to the person you dream of becoming. As you seek to climb the Value Appreciation Ladder, you grow your appreciation for your own value and your passion for delivering value to others.

When you are able to be secure and confident in who you are, people are better able to see who you are and decide if you're someone they want to follow. If you see people put off by something you do, ask yourself why that is and if you can correct something. That feedback may be essential to crafting your value and learning how to monetize it.

If your income is dependent on you being yourself, it acts as a great check on any temptation to be disingenuous. The more you are yourself, the more likely you are to see the returns. Appreciate your value.

Habit 4: The Mastermind Habit: Find Your Influential Relationships

Ask not what your connections can do for you but what you can do for your connections. Start with service—remember to use the

Service-to-Value Lever (Chapter 9). You can grow better when you have others pulling you up instead of pushing you down.

Find people who can teach you what they know. Pursue those relationships that will save you from learning every hard lesson yourself. It's okay to be willing to learn. But you can avoid a lot of mistakes by learning from your peers in your field instead of having to learn everything on your own.

Don't allow people to think you are someone you aren't. I promise that as you grow, you'll continue to see people taking an interest in you and who you will be. Soon you'll find your chosen financial family and be making money easy.

Habit 5: The Magnetic Habit: Become an Enrollment Artist

Enrollment is an art. I live my life ready to make a connection with anyone. That's why I was so excited about LinkedIn early on. The more excited you are about what you're doing, the more people will be excited to work with you.

Connections are where the seeds of a relationship happen. But enrollment is where the real magic happens. Enrollment happens when you enlist others in your vision. Your consistency, passion, and ability to achieve your goals will also attract them. Eventually people will follow your lead, and you'll see a team forming.

But enrollment never ends. It constantly grows your following. That growth comes from your ability to lead and lead well. Follow the Personal Power Principle: *How well you lead yourself determines your personal power to lead others.* When you enroll others, you give people the opportunity to join you in your vision and pursue it together.

Habit 6: The Mobility Habit: Delegate to Empower Others

If you want something done right, do it yourself. If you want something done great, do it with others. Every day you have opportunities to delegate if you are willing to let go and take them. Finding the balance takes time, but it makes a difference.

When you leverage the strengths of others, you can find ways to cover your weaknesses. That is how a strong team is built.

I have never known of something great that was made in just a day. It takes time and effort, but it pays off. Delegation allows your team to become *us* instead of *me*. It's still your vision, but that doesn't mean you have to walk alone.

And if you do start a business, resist the temptation to be a helicopter entrepreneur. The Mobility Habit will allow you to lead your team to overcome obstacles, adapt to change, and grow faster than your competitors. It can take you from good to great—and beyond.

Habit 7: The Mastery Habit: Cultivate Your Money Wisdom

The Mastery Habit is all about learning, so make the commitment to grow your money know-how a little more every day. Practice the habits daily to increase the likelihood of becoming a money master. The Mastery Habit is all about learning. You have the potential to be the best and brightest you can be, but you must be willing to learn.

Whenever you fall short or miss a deadline, or things don't go the way you plan—learn from it. Every step you take is an opportunity to adapt and overcome. Remember that the master of any subject puts in the work. They are disciplined and know their stuff. They learned what works and what doesn't and have earned their education through trial and error.

Financial literacy is critical to creating financial peace. Focus on the basics of the Financial Knowledge Flow: Learn. Share. Teach. You are never done growing! In fact, I still have a long way to go. But that is the exciting part. Every day you get to learn a little more. And as you learn more, you open yourself up to earn more.

Now, let's see how well the habits are already part of the fabric of your life. This will help you see where you are strongest right now and where you need to put the most focused effort to grow.

Take the following simple assessment to discover your Money Habits score.

The Money Habit Assessment

Give each statement below a score of 1 to 10.

(1 = "I completely disagree" and 10 = "I strongly agree")

To what extent do the following statements accurately describe you right now?

The Mindset Habit

1. I live life with a grateful heart, express my gratitude often, and practice gratitude daily. _____

2. I give generously of what I have to help others. _____

3. I think in an abundant way that attracts money to me, like a magnet. _____

Total Score: _____

The Mapping Habit

4. I am intentional about planning my future and not simply repeating the past. _____

5. I have a clear money vision with real numbers and a practical plan to achieve it. _____

6. More than just money, my plans include living a rich and meaningful life. _____

Total Score: _____

The Monetizing Habit

7. I have learned to appreciate my own value and can easily explain what it is. _____

8. I know how to package my value to make it appealing to the marketplace. _____

9. I regularly protect my value from negative perspectives, fear, and self-doubt. _____

Total Score: _____

The Mastermind Habit

10. I start by thinking of how I can serve others,
    not how they can serve me. _____

11. I intentionally cultivate relationships to surround
    myself with my chosen financial community. _____

12. I regularly ask questions of people to learn
    how I might best serve their needs. _____

Total Score: _____

The Magnetic Habit

13. I am passionate about what I do,
    and everyone knows it! _____

14. I study leadership to increase my influence
    and enroll others in my vision. _____

15. I first lead myself well so I can be
    best positioned to enroll others. _____

Total Score: _____

The Mobility Habit

16. I quickly and easily delegate to leverage
    the strengths of others. _____

17. I know my worth and delegate anything
    that does not deliver that value to me. _____

18. I am a master at mobilizing my team to
    deliver their best and scale our results. _____

Total Score: _____

The Mastery Habit

19. I regularly seek ways to learn
    more so I can earn more. _____

20. I engage in money conversations and enjoy
    talking about money with others. _____

21. I actively seek to learn, share, and teach
    so money knowledge freely flows. _____

Total Score: _____

Write your scores for each habit in the corresponding blank in the following pyramid:

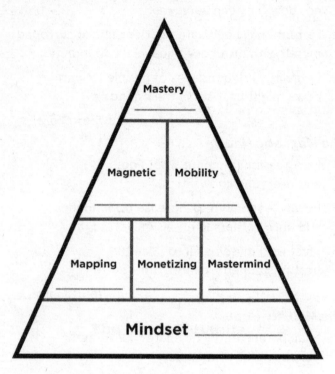

Which habit has the highest score?

_____

Which habit do you need to focus on next?

_____

Take Action: Based on what you've read, what practical actions will you take next to help you grow in your next Habit Focus Area?

1. _____

2. _____

3. _____

NOW . . . GO MAKE MORE MONEY!

Thank you for joining me on this money journey. Your willingness to enroll in my Meaningful Mission means a lot to me. And I hope it has helped you push through the resistance to find greater clarity for your own Money Story.

I want you to know that you are always welcome to join me on this journey. So please tag me on your favorite social media platforms and let me know how this book helped you.

Your journey is just getting started. There will be setbacks. Life happens, but you'll be okay. Challenging seasons come and go, but when you are willing to learn and grow through them, you can embrace the opportunities available from them.

Remember, you are enough *and* you are becoming more. Now go, live a richer life!

Find more free resources to accelerate your growth and make money easy at MakeMoneyEasyBook.com.

ENDNOTES

INTRODUCTION

1.   Emily Batdorf, "Living Paycheck to Paycheck Statistics 2024," Forbes, April 2, 2024, https://www.forbes.com/advisor/banking/living-paycheck-to-paycheck-statistics-2024/; Andrew Lisa, "Retirement 2024: 28% of Americans Have $0 Saved for Their Golden Years," Yahoo! Finance, March 12, 2024, https://finance.yahoo.com/news/retirement-2024-28-americans-0-110151188.html; Lane Gillespie, "Bankrate's Annual Emergency Fund Report," Bankrate, June 20, 2024, https://www.bankrate.com/banking/savings/emergency-savings-report/#job-loss.

CHAPTER 3

1.   Lewis Howes, "Train Your Brain to Do the Hard Things in Life for Success!" Katy Milkman and Lewis Howes, YouTube, August 25, 2021, https://www.youtube.com/watch?v=f3c5FO9WTs0.

CHAPTER 4

1.   Lewis Howes, "Stop Trying to Get Rich and Focus on This Instead!" Jay Shetty and Lewis Howes, YouTube, July 27, 2022, https://www.youtube.com/watch?v=dBFz0GgC9UQ.

2.   Lewis Howes, "'I Am Wealthy'—3 Steps to Manifest Money, Success and Happiness!" Ken Honda and Lewis Howes, YouTube, October 19, 2022, https://www.youtube.com/watch?v=rHjolP34pyc.

3.   Ibid.

CHAPTER 5

1. Bob Goff, *Love Does: Discover a Secretly Incredible Life in an Ordinary World* (Nashville, TN: Thomas Nelson, 2012).

2. Lisa Respers France, "Jim Carrey's Inspiring Commencement Speech," CNN, May 28, 2014, https://www.cnn.com/2014/05/28/showbiz/celebrity-news-gossip/jim-carrey-commencement-speech/index.html.

3. Lewis Howes, "Stop Trying to Get Rich and Focus on This Instead!" Jay Shetty and Lewis Howes, YouTube, July 27, 2022, https://www.youtube.com/watch?v=dBFz0GgC9UQ.

4. Lewis Howes, "Make Money and Make an Impact," Tim Sykes and Lewis Howes, YouTube, January 23, 2017, https://www.youtube.com/watch?v=Tsu_YGpSAbE.

CHAPTER 6

1. Lewis Howes, "This Yale Professor Reveals the Science on How to Be Happy Everyday," Laurie Santos and Lewis Howes, YouTube, June 1, 2020, https://www.youtube.com/watch?v=44ECNxPIVx8&t=737s.

2. Lewis Howes, "The Most Eye-Opening Speech on Why You're Not Happy in Life," Ed Mylett and Lewis Howes, YouTube, June 8, 2022, https://www.youtube.com/watch?v=RrSBoHAfZiA&t=2048s.

3. Ibid.

4. Lewis Howes, "Head of TED: Increase Your Happiness & Abundance! The Simple Strategy to Reaching Billions," Chris Anderson and Lewis Howes, YouTube, March 6, 2024, https://www.youtube.com/watch?v=2INEmQ5Y4eg.

5. Lewis Howes, "Manifest Money! Creator of *The Secret* on Making Money with the Law of Attraction," Rhonda Byrne and Lewis Howes, YouTube, January 15, 2024, https://www.youtube.com/watch?v=Nmibkd2Vp2U.

6. Ibid.

7. Ibid.

8. Alan Watts, "Work and Play," The Library of Consciousness, 1972, https://www.organism.earth/library/document/essential-lectures-7.

9. Lewis Howes, "'I Am Wealthy'—3 Steps to Manifest Money, Success and Happiness!" Ken Honda and Lewis Howes, YouTube, October 19, 2022, https://www.youtube.com/watch?v=rHjolP34pyc.

10. Ibid.

CHAPTER 7

1. Richard Batts, "Why Most New Year's Resolutions Fail," *Lead Read Today*, Fisher College of Business, Ohio State University, February 2, 2023, https://fisher.osu.edu/blogs/leadreadtoday/why-most-new-years-resolutions-fail#:~:text=Researchers%20suggest%20that%20only%209,fail%20at%20New%20Year%27s%20resolutions.

2. Paulo Coelho, "1 Minute Reading: The Fisherman and the Businessman," Paulo Coelho, *Stories and Reflections*, March 16, 2021, https://paulocoelhoblog.com/2015/09/04/the-fisherman-and-the-businessman/.

3. Lewis Howes, "Neuroscientist Reveals How to Never Lack Willpower Again!" Kelly McGonigal and Lewis Howes, YouTube, September 18, 2022, https://www.youtube.com/watch?v=mV3aoHuS29o&list=PLMG5w22POeeykqONbfGi00m4AqxhnzmWc&index=166.

4. Ibid.

5. Lewis Howes, "The Key Signs You're Going to Become Successful and Wealthy," Patrick Bet-David and Lewis Howes, YouTube, August 12, 2020, https://www.youtube.com/watch?v=6GmTlmpg4Ho.

CHAPTER 8

1. Lewis Howes, "Allyson Felix on Breaking Olympic Records, Shattering Stereotypes and Unleashing Greatness," Allyson Felix and Lewis Howes, YouTube, June 19, 2023, https://www.youtube.com/watch?v=QtWdusC09Do.

2. Lewis Howes, "If You Want to Become a Millionaire, Follow These Steps!" Rachel Rodgers and Lewis Howes, YouTube, November 10, 2021, https://www.youtube.com/watch?v=1lMkLtjqaps.

CHAPTER 9

1. Zig Ziglar, Secrets of Closing the Sale (Grand Rapids, MI: Revell, 2022).

CHAPTER 10

1. Howes, "The Most Eye-Opening Speech."

2. Lewis Howes, "How I Went from Broke to Millionaire in 90 Days!" Grant Cardone and Lewis Howes, YouTube, February 17, 2021, https://www.youtube.com/watch?v=IM6I-ejDlzo&t=909s.

3. John Maxwell, Goodreads, accessed March 8, 2024, https://www.goodreads.com/quotes/479285-he-who-thinks-he-leads-but-has-no-followers-is.

4.   Wayne Dyer, BrainyQuote, accessed March 11, 2024, https://www
     .brainyquote.com/quotes/wayne_dyer_154410.

CHAPTER 11

1.   Lewis Howes, "If You Want to Become a Millionaire, Follow These
     Steps!" Rachel Rodgers and Lewis Howes, YouTube, November 10,
     2021, https://www.youtube.com/watch?v=1lMkLtjqaps.

CHAPTER 12

1.   Emily Batdorf, "Living Paycheck to Paycheck Statistics 2024," *Forbes
     Advisor*, April 2, 2024, https://www.forbes.com/advisor/banking/
     living-paycheck-to-paycheck-statistics-2024/#how-many-americans
     -are-living-paycheck-to-paycheck.

2.   Andrew Lisa, "Retirement 2024: 28% of Americans Have $0 Saved for
     Their Golden Years," Yahoo Finance, March 12, 2024, https://finance
     .yahoo.com/news/retirement-2024-28-americans-0-110151188.html.

3.   Lane Gillespie, "Bankrate's 2024 Annual Emergency Savings Report,"
     Bankrate, June 30, 2024, https://www.bankrate.com/banking/savings
     /emergency-savings-report/#job-loss.

4.   Dave Ramsey, "If You Want to Become a Millionaire Watch This!"
     Rev.com, https://www.rev.com/transcript-editor/shared/io-_yv8pxco
     URvZN7C9xgYHXHJkq67xtEYzPB4KcHDti2b6E2zqf5SOXwf0cUXLSf
     LkUJUWHFW2AitvPfXknfZ9QMr0?loadFrom=SharedLink.

5.   Lewis Howes, "Be Financially Free and Pay Yourself First," David Bach
     and Lewis Howes, YouTube, May 1, 2019, https://www.youtube.com/
     watch?v=ZUObyxtHO50.

ACKNOWLEDGMENTS

Much like my previous book *The Greatness Mindset*, I think it is important for us to honor our younger selves—the ones who entered this world and bravely navigated its many uncertainties.

To the child in me, who watched in awe as my father tipped with $2 bills: Thank you for teaching me to see the beauty in the small, the unique, and the unexpected. Your wonder and curiosity remind me that every one of us has something special to bring to the world. You set the foundation for the resilience and creativity I would later need.

To my 24-year-old self, broke in every sense of the word—financially, physically, and emotionally—while living on my sister's couch: Thank you for your unwavering commitment to impact over income, Meaningful Mission over money, and growth over comfort. Your grit, even when the road seemed endless, paved the way for this moment. You didn't give up when life felt impossible, and for that, I owe you everything.

Both versions of me, in their own ways, faced uncertainty, pain, and loss yet still sought healing, peace, and truth. You carried me to this season of life. Your courage, your persistence, and your faith in a brighter future made this book—and the life I now live—possible. For that, I am eternally grateful.

To my wife, Martha Higareda: Thank you for being my rock, my confidante, and my greatest supporter. You not only see my vision—you amplify it with your unwavering belief in me and the mission we share. Your love is a constant reminder that the true richness of life comes from relationships built on authenticity, mutual growth, and unshakable trust.

You inspire me daily with your wisdom, kindness, and ability to see beauty and possibility in every moment. Whether we're dreaming big, tackling challenges, or simply enjoying the quiet moments together, your presence fills my life with joy and meaning. Thank you for walking this path by my side, for fully embracing who I am, and for being my greatest partner in this incredible journey. I love you more than words can ever express.

To my mother: Your unwavering strength and compassion continue to inspire me. You've shown me the importance of investing not only in health and family but also in the values that truly matter. Your love is a reminder that wealth is not just what we hold in our hands but what we give from our hearts.

To my late father: Your lessons live on in everything I do. You gave me the passion and confidence to take risks, to dream boldly, and to trust myself enough to become an entrepreneur. Every time I open my wallet and see the $2 bills you loved so much, I think of you. Those bills remind me of the uniqueness we each bring to the world and the mindset you instilled in me to always see possibility and potential. Thank you for your love, wisdom, and belief in me.

To my siblings, Chris, Heidi, and Katherine: You have been my constant source of accountability, encouragement, and love. Through every challenge, you remind me that success is most meaningful when it's shared with those who matter most.

To Team Greatness: Thank you for your passion, vision, and tireless dedication. This journey wouldn't be possible without your commitment to bringing big ideas to life. Together, we are building something that impacts lives and inspires others to align their purpose with financial freedom.

To Matt Cesaratto and Sarah Livingstone: Your loyalty and hard work are invaluable. You've shown me that partnerships rooted in trust and shared goals are among the greatest assets anyone can have.

Special thanks to my writing partner Bill Blankschaen and his StoryBuilders team for bringing this book to life. You helped turn ideas into actionable insights, creating a resource that I hope will change lives.

To Lisa Cheng, Monica O'Connor, Brittany Muller, Lizzi Marshall, Diane Hill, Lindsay McGinty, Patty Gift, Reid Tracy, and the team at Hay House: Your expertise and dedication elevate this project. I'm grateful for your commitment to delivering messages that matter and helping readers transform their lives.

To the coaches, teachers, and mentors who shaped me: Thank you for sharing your wisdom and empowering me to think bigger. You've taught me the value of a strong mindset as the foundation for a truly abundant life.

To the guests of *The School of Greatness* podcast: Your stories and perspectives have enriched not only this book but the lives of countless listeners, viewers, and readers. Thank you for sharing your journeys and inspiring others to align their missions with their money stories.

To my readers and supporters: Thank you for taking this step toward healing your relationship with money. Your courage to embrace growth and create a meaningful life reminds me why I do what I do.

Finally, to anyone who has ever felt stuck or trapped by their financial circumstances: This book is for you. May it serve as a guide to help you break free, build the life you deserve, and discover the true power of financial peace and freedom.

ABOUT THE AUTHOR

Lewis Howes is the *New York Times* best-selling author of *The Greatness Mindset* and *The School of Greatness*, a keynote speaker, and an industry-leading show host. Howes is a two-sport All-American athlete, former professional football player, and member of the USA Men's National Handball Team. His show *The School of Greatness* is one of the top podcasts in the world with over 1 billion downloads. He was recognized by the White House and President Obama as one of the top 100 entrepreneurs in the country under 30. Lewis has been featured on *Ellen*, the *TODAY* show, *The New York Times*, *People*, *Forbes*, *Fast Company*, *ESPN*, *Entrepreneur*, *Sports Illustrated*, and *Men's Health*. Visit: **LewisHowes.com**